ELIMINATION

THE 'ZZ TOP' STORY BY DAVID THOMAS

Omnibus Press

London/New York/Sydney/Cologne

© 1985 Omnibus Press
(A Division of Book Sales Limited)

Edited by Chris Charlesworth.
Art Direction by Mike Bell.
Book Designed by Rory Matthews.
Picture Research by Valerie Boyd.

ISBN 0.7119.0718.8
Order No. OP 43447

Exclusive distributors:
Book Sales Limited
78 Newman Street, London W1P 3LA, UK.
Cherry Lane Books
PO Box 430, Port Chester, NY 10573, USA.
Omnibus Press
GPO Box 3304, Sydney, NSW 2001, Australia.
To the Music Trade only:
Music Sales Limited
78 Newman Street, London W1P 3LA, UK.

Cover photo credits:
Front: Rex Features.
Back: Justin Thomas

Typeset by Pinnacle and Futurafoto.

Printed in England by
Wm. Clowes (Beccles) Limited, London & Beccles.

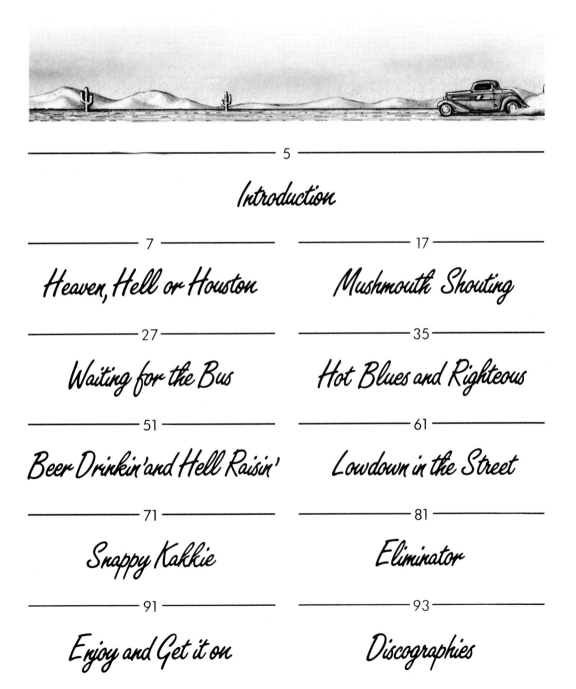

Contents

RETNA

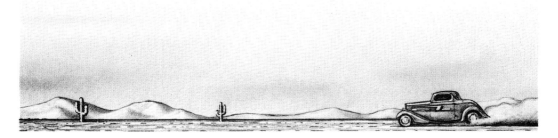

Introduction

August 25th, 1984, was a momentous day in the annals of British rock music. *BBC2*, the state-run "alternative/minority" viewing channel, offered a full fourteen-and-a-quarter hours of non-stop rock and pop. Beginning at 3.15 pm, *Rock Around The Clock*, only the second event of its kind to be screened in the UK, was the nearest the country had ever come to the full, twenty-four hours a day saturation coverage afforded by America's MTV. But while MTV concentrates almost exclusively on videos, *Rock Around The Clock* served up a more esoteric potpourri of concert footage (The Cure, Simple Minds, The Pretenders), documentary (The Doors, Aztec Camera, The Police), and film (*The Buddy Holly Story, FM, The Last Waltz*). Conventional videos took a secondary (and, in retrospect, ill-deserved) backseat to the main action. Michael Jackson's *Thriller* was screened in its entirety, and nestling away in the schedules, at 11.26 pm to be precise, was a triumvirate of videos which, prior to screening, had many a viewer scratching their heads and asking, 'Who the hell is *that*?' The group was ZZ Top.

The videos were 'Gimme All Your Loving', 'Sharp Dressed Man' and 'Legs', all three tracks from the Texan outfit's current 'Eliminator' album, highly acclaimed across the Atlantic, but which caused less than a ripple in Europe.

All three had already been screened in Britain, of course; separately they had appeared on various rock shows, but to muted applause and little commercial effect. ZZ Top themselves had something of a local reputation. A short British tour the previous autumn attracted good notices and excellent crowds. But on the vinyl front 'Eliminator' was small fry indeed compared to the current obsessions of the British record buying public. Number one single that weekend was 'Careless Whimper' by Whamboy George Michael. Below that, Black Lace's novelty party-pooper 'Agadoo', Frankie Goes To Hollywood, psychedelic parodist Neil and the eternal Laura Branigan jockeyed for position with Howard Jones' claim that he'd like to get to know us all well; most right-thinking folk above the age of 14 could scarcely think of anything they'd like less.

The album chart was little better. The latest in a perennial line of TV advertised hits compilation albums, 'Now That's What I Call Music, Volume 397' was at the top, Lionel Ritchie, Nik Kershaw, Michael Jackson and that accursed Howard Jones filled the next few positions.

But then came *Rock Around The Clock*. At 11.26, 'Gimme All Your Lovin' kicked into gear. The album from which the song came stood at number 75 in the British chart. Fifteen minutes later, as the last seconds of 'Legs' died away, it

was still at number 75, but only for as long as it took the nation's record stores to open. Within ten days, 'Eliminator' had risen to number 12. A week after that it was into the Top 10. It has stayed there ever since.

ZZ Top's European success, of course, is nothing compared to the band's popularity in their homeland. At the end of December 1984, 'Eliminator' boasted worldwide sales of almost eight million, but the European market accounted for less than a third of that. Their popularity in Europe was still new. When ZZ Top toured in the autumn of 1983, neither their fame nor their music had spread much beyond a select elite, although perhaps that undermines a following which, in Britain at least, was strong enough to see the band pack out some of the biggest venues in both London and the provinces. If they toured today, however, it is doubtful whether there would be more than half a dozen venues in the entire country remotely capable of holding them.

What is it about ZZ Top which has, after more than fifteen years together, seen them finally take the world by the scruff of its neck?

Their music? Even the band themselves would admit that, new technology notwithstanding, the difference between the songs on 'Eliminator' and the songs on 'ZZ Top's First Album' is negligible; a little more commercial, perhaps, a little more pop orientated, but it's the same three chords, the same ethic of sex and drugs and rock 'n' roll, the same li'l ol' boogie band from Texas.

Their image? Beards and funny hats are hardly a priority for the identikit teenage idol, cuddly or not. In fact, Frank still loves to reiterate the story of how, one day in the lobby of New York's Gramercy Park Hotel, 'The elevator opens and this guy gets out. He's wearin' hot pants, black fishnet tights, a feather boa and make-up and he's carrying a bullwhip over his shoulder and two *leatherette* women on his arms. He marches through the lobby and I'm elbowin' Dusty, goin' 'Goddamn, look at *that*.' And we look around - and everyone in the whole lobby is staring at *us!*'

Or perhaps it's the videos which have made all the difference, that trio of very funny, very clever vignettes which feature girls, which feature cars, which feature an ordinary guy, and which, with one flash of a customised key ring, promise that all this could be yours! Just be in the right place at the right time, and hope that there's three weird looking hombres somewhere around to keep everything running smooth.

But most likely, it's none of these things and it was ZZ themselves who, thanks to a lot of hard work and not a little luck, found *themselves* in the right place at the right time. There'd been a big gap at the top of the rock hierarchy for a long time, just crying out for someone to come along and fill it. ZZ Top filled it.... And how.

CHAPTER 1.

Heaven, Hell or Houston

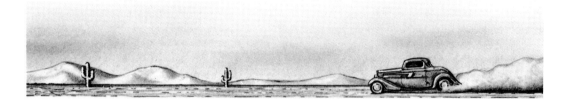

Texas; the Lone Star state. With two hundred and sixty-seven thousand square miles at its disposal, it's the second largest state in the whole of America - Alaska is the biggest. You could fit the United Kingdom into Texas three times, and still have room left over to graze some cattle. Paradoxically, Texas boasts a population three times *less* than the U.K.; they prefer to give the land over to farming and oil, which Texans go for in a big way.

There again, Texans go in for most things in a big way. Including Texas. 'To give you some idea of at what an early age people start bragging about Texas, I remember my mama telling me and my little sister: 'Y'll be good children and when you grow up and die, instead of goin' to Heaven you'll stay in Texas,' Billy Gibbons likes to say. That, or maybe he'll give you a fact that would tend to open most people's eyes about just how vast the State is.' The other day we had to go to a place called Dalhart, Texas. Dalhart is closer to twenty-two other States than it is to Austin, which is its own State capital!'.

It is that sort of imagery which, he claims, ZZ Top are trying to capture in their music. The Texas of open roads and empty deserts, tumbleweed and mountains, the Texas which is just an enchillada's throw across from Mexico and whose heritage is part Latino, part cowboy and, if you explore past the south-west corner of Houston, Billy G.'s home town, is as sin-infested as they come. The Texas where the barbecue stands cook on Sundays and have a good ol' time while everyone else is praying in church.

But most of all ZZ recreate the Texas of Bob Wills and Ernest Tubb, of Henry Thomas and Bobby Bland. The lone star state has a musical heritage as big as its heart, a multi-racial, multi-lingual tradition which began with Western swing, rocketed through country and gospel, took a swipe at soul, and ended up with the greatest rhythm 'n' blues scene in the world. Moon Mullican - the King of the hillbilly piano players and a major influence on Jerry Lee Lewis - was a Texan. So was Huey P. Meaux, Houston's answer to Phil Spector and the man behind every local talent from Jivin' Gene to Sunny & The Sun-liners, Roy Head to Dougie Sahm & The Sir Douglas Quintet... 'She's About A Mover', 'At The Crossroads', 'Mendocino'. B.J. Thomas came from Houston, Janis Joplin came from Port Arthur, and The Bobby Fuller Four came from El Paso. They might have achieved fame and notor-iety via Los Angeles and The Clash, but 'I Fought The Law' was Texan through and through.

'There's a tremendous musical heritage which dates back to the fifties,' Billy Gibbons says of Houston. 'It was a major R&B market. Ray Charles to this day will swear by Texas musicians. Little Richard picked up his entire band out of

Houston. Duke-Peacock Records were based in Houston.'

And, of course, Billy himself was born there, in the suburb of Tanglewood, on December 12, 1949. His father, Fred Gibbons, had lived there since the thirties, leaving his native New York home and his English-born parents for the homeland of his first wife. Her family owned a string of cinemas in Houston, the *Iris* chain. Fred himself worked in Hollywood for a while, on the other side of the silver screen, conducting and arranging film scores. He conducted the Houston Philharmonic Orchestra as well, and worked with the big Las Vegas showcase superstars.

It's this latter involvement which Billy remembers best; that and the contacts his dad made as they drove through the desert from Houston to Vegas, watching the arid landscape flash by. Or the occasion when Fred flew the whole family up to Vegas for a birthday party at the Tropicana for actor Dick Powell, best known today for his juvenile leads (opposite Ruby Keeler) in the old Busby Berkeley spectaculars.

Billy and sister Pam were sent to play by the swimming pool where they met none other than Humphrey Bogart. He bought them cokes, he talked to them, and when Fred Gibbons came to reclaim his offspring, Humph gave him that crooked smile and said: 'These yours? They're nice kids.'

Billy grew up surrounded by classical music, but he never really liked it. Neither did he care much for the country music which gushed forth from radio stations right across the dial. But then he saw Elvis Presley on the *Ed Sullivan Show*. The date was September 9, 1956, and the King was making his debut on a show whose host once remarked, 'I wouldn't touch Elvis Presley with a big stick, and then had to pay fifty thousand bucks when the ratings war dictated he eat his

Below: Beer drinkers and guitar eaters.
Right: Billy Gibbons.

ROSS HALFIN

DAVID REDFERN

DAVID REDFERN

Invasion had already been assimilated into the system; the San Francisco explosion was still to come. Into this void came the garage bands, High School Heroes with acne and scratchy guitars who aped current chart toppers, played squeaky organs with one finger and, in Texas, had names like ? And The Mysterions, The Cynics, Kenny & The Kasuals, The Bad Seeds and The 4 Frogs. Their sound was an amalgamation of fantasy ('Anyone can be a Rock 'n' Roll star...') and reality ('.. well, almost anyone'). Arch critic Lester Bangs surmised that '...The greatest garage bands could barely play. (Therefore) we may assume not only that virtuosity has nothing to do with form, but also that the Utopian dream of every man an artist can come true right here, in our suburban land of opportunity.'

In late 1966 The Coachmen decided to put this theory to the test. A hundred miles upstate, The 13th Floor Elevators were spearheading

Above: Billy: Move On Down The Line.

Texas' answer to the garage psychedelics with 'You're Gonna Miss Me', a regional hit par excellence. Based in Austin, The Elevators were forever on the verge of breaking nationally, and that despite the perpetual attentions of federal narcotic agents who pursued the group everywhere before hounding the band's already unstable vocalist, Roky Ericson, into a mental institution for three years.

At the time of their emergence, however, the Elevators were truly leaders of the pack, screaming and screeching their acid drenched variations on a theme from The Yardbirds and corrupting the morals of a thousand young

Coachmen. Billy Gibbons, immediately impressed by The Elevators, swiftly persuaded his fellow band members to take off their soul shoes and get into some honest psychedelia instead. And just to convince them further, he presented them with '99th Floor', a tribute to The Elevators and the product of a high school mathematics lesson.

Right: The Tibetan look.
Below: Billy with double-neck guitar.

LONDON FEATURES INTERNATIONAL

'How The Elevators came up with their sound no-one knows to this day,' says Billy. 'They were from a dead little tourist town in central Texas. There was nothing there at all. All we know is that they drank Listerine Mouth Wash.

'We made the jump from soul band to psychedelic band early in the summer of 1967. That's when the line was drawn. All of a sudden, nobody could understand what we were doing...We said 'Hey! We're on to something. They hate us, let's go for it!'

'The *New Musical Express* described '99th Floor' as 'a collision of Them's 'Gloria' and The Elevators' 'You're Gonna Miss Me'... (It) remains a pinnacle of '60s garage punk, a stabbing riff of fuzz Vox organ and tinny, /needling guitar. ' Billy was later quoted as claiming the guitar solo was inspired by 'the groovy lead' on 'Sunshine Superman', a 1966 number one for Donovan.

Changing their name to The Moving Sidewalks, Billy and Co. entered into a period of intensive gigging, hitting every night-club that would have them in Texas and Louisiana. Once '99th Floor' had topped the local Houston chart, their workload increased and by the time the Wand/Sceptre label picked up the single for nationwide distribution, The Moving Sidewalks were playing as often as five nights a week earning between eight hundred and a thousand dollars per show. And, from all accounts, they deserved it. Billy frequently set the stage on fire as part of his act, while strobe lights and fire-cracker explosions were all part of a night's work for the group's road crew. So was being on guard for accidents, such as the one which almost blew Sidewalks' drummer Dan Mitchell's head off while the band were supporting Ten Years After. TYA's Alvin Lee and Leo Lyons rushed Dan to hospital and must have been dumbfounded when the attendants who greeted them initially refused to have anything to do with the casualty because he had long hair. According to all concerned, having long hair in Texas was to be dicing with death - Billy's mother refused point blank to allow her son to even contemplate growing his locks, and it wasn't unusual for her to ban his friends from entering the house for fear that one of her friends might associate her per-

sonally with the hirsute vision presented by Billy's friends.

Domestic respectability, however, played no part in Billy's music. The Moving Sidewalks became one of the Lone Star state's biggest attractions, and never so much as when the story went around that they had received the approval of none other than Jimi Hendrix, then just breaking in the United States as the biggest black artist of that - or any other - decade.

Legend has it that The Moving Sidewalks, riding high with '99th Floor', were one of several local bands selected to open for Hendrix when he played four shows (two in Houston, one each in Dallas and San Antonio) in the neighbour-hood.

Impressed by the skills of the Sidewalks' guitarist, Hendrix invited the band to play the rest of the tour as his own personal guests. Then, when he got back to New York, and was guesting on the Johnny Carson hosted *Tonight* show, Hendrix actually described Billy as the best up 'n' coming guitarist in the country.

It is a tale which Billy has never tired of reiterating. 'The first time I heard about Hendrix, I read about his Monterey appearance. So I got someone to send a copy of 'Are You Experienced' over from England. I took it over to this girl's house. She was this really heavy soul chick, so she put it on thinking she was going to be hearing Wilson Pickett or something. We just sat there thinking: 'This ain't Stax Records!' I was 17 and that was just what the doctor ordered.

'Jimi and I got along fine, real fine,' Billy told *Rolling Stone*. 'Of course, I was only 17 at the time and a real impressionable sort, but when I first met him I was floored. He'd dyed his hair orange and I'd never seen anything like it before. He really taught me a lot about guitar.'

On another occasion, he told *Sounds* that the first time he met Hendrix 'He was lying on the floor with his head shaved bald at the back, with a peroxide strip going through the remainder. And he was just laying there playing this unbelievable, undying string of riffs. And he said 'What d'you think? and I said 'I've never heard that song before,' and he said, 'No, I mean what d'you think of the haircut?'

ROSS HALFIN/REPFOTO LONDON

Obviously Billy's memory plays some strange tricks over the years. But wait, the plot thickens. Widespread as Billy's fond reminiscences are, equally widespread are the tales of how The Sidewalks never toured with Hendrix, that their engagement was confined to just those four dates in Texas. And that Jimi, when he returned to New York, did *not* mention Billy on the *Tonight* show, but may have given the Sidewalks a name-check on a radio interview around the same time.

But most mysterious of all is the story of Billy's famed Hendrix guitar, a vivid pink Fender Stratocaster which, he claims, was a personal gift from the Master himself. And once again, he has photographic evidence to back it up: a Polaroid snap of Jimi, the Sidewalks and, dead centre, a Strat. Only the Strat wasn't pink.

None of Billy's friends, supposedly, remember hearing of Hendrix ever giving Billy a guitar, and the common consensus of opinion is that the

fable, like so much of Billy's personal mythology, has its roots in two separate incidents. The first is Jimi's attempts to swap his Fender twelve-string for a black Les Paul owned by a member of another band on the Texas bill, John Perelen of Neil Ford and The Fanatics. The second is that Billy, in the studio with the Sidewalks one day, decided his customary Les Paul sound wasn't right for the track. He wanted a 'Hendrix' sound, and bade one of the roadies to fetch him his Stratocaster - which just happened to be pink. Superimpose one tale on to the other, and from little acorns...

Less open to controversy (and, strangely enough, less documented) is Billy's encounter with Eric Clapton. It occurred during Cream's Farewell tour of America in 1969: the Sidewalks were rehearsing in Richard Ames' Catacombs Club and Clapton just happened to drop by in time to witness the Sidewalks powering through their own frenetic version of Cream's own 'Crossroads' showstopper. At the end of the song Clapton walked over to the stage, shook Billy's hand, and the two of them spent the rest of the afternoon talking about the blues.

The Moving Sidewalks never managed a follow-up to '99th Floor', despite remaining with the Wand label for one further single. Or maybe even that was an ill-omened move. While Wand's sister company, Scepter, had a guaranteed chart act in Dionne Warwick, Wand managed only half a dozen hits in more than two decades of trying, and that despite being the first company to pick up on The Isley Brothers! Other Wand acts, like Chuck Jackson, The Joe Jeffrey Group, The Independents and Maxine Brown (who scored with a classic rendering of 'Oh No Not My Baby'), hit once, maybe twice, but Wand was *not* a label with a

good track record. And The Moving Sidewalks' 'Need Me' single was never likely to rectify that state of affairs.

The group returned to the cosy confines of the Houston-based Tantara independent who had released the original '99th Floor', but even their muse was doomed. A witheringly psychedelic retread of The Beatles' 'I Wanna Hold Your Hand' barely sold even to the group's hard-core fans, while the band's album, 'Flash', was to ultimately prove more useful to sundry retrospective repackagers once Billy hit the heights with ZZ Top than to The Moving Sidewalks - or The Electric Sidewalks, as Billy has since claimed they became after changing their name at the suggestion of...Jimi Hendrix. 'Flash' has been reissued twice, once in 1983 by a European company which picked up on the now discarded Tantara label identity, and once by the French Eva label, who retitled it '99th Floor' and added four earlier, single-only, cuts to the original LP.

The band's final single was 'Flashbacks', a cut from the album and one which coincided with the death throes of The Moving Sidewalks. Aged just 19, the Sidewalks, like the rest of their generation, finally won recognition from Uncle Sam. Sure you can vote, sure you can screw, sure you can drink. And if you're real good and don't do anything silly like enrol in University, you can have an expenses-paid trip out to Viet-Nam.

Billy was one of the silly ones. Quick as a flash he enrolled in the University of Texas, studying art. Sidewalks' drummer Dan Mitchell followed suit, but Tom Moore the keyboard player, did heed his country's call. In his stead came Lanier Greig, late of Neil Ford and The Fanatics. But after bassist Don Summers fell foul to patriotism as well, there seemed to be little alternative but to call it a day. The Sidewalks never moved again.

CHAPTER 2.

Mushmouth Shouting

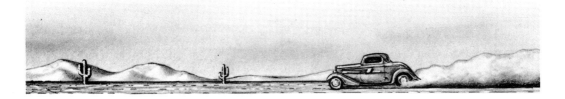

Joe 'Dusty' Hill was born in Dallas. His mother was an accomplished, if unambitious, singer, a fan of Elvis, Little Richard, and Lightnin' Hopkins; his step-father worked on the Ford production line. Dusty's biggest influence, though, was big brother Rocky, a blues guitarist whom Dusty to this day maintains is the more talented of the two.

'When I was eight I got a guitar for Christmas. Rocky got a bicycle. We did a swap; Rocky learned to play guitar, I almost broke my neck'.

Surrendering the joys of cycling for a microphone, Dusty and Rocky took to playing afternoons in the cafes where their mother worked. At least, they were cafes in the afternoon. At night they were beer joints.

Dusty's forte was an Elvis Presley impersonation; Rocky's was to ape Scotty Moore, Presley's long-serving guitarist. When Rocky decided to form a band, it was only natural that little brother Billy should follow him into its ranks, picking up a bass guitar along the way for no better reason than the fact that Rocky had already recruited a guitarist and drummer.

This first band, The Starliners, gradually metamorphosed into The Deadbeats, and Dusty set about living up to that name with a vengeance. In summer school gigs always took precedence over school work; during the regular term a weekend trip to Tennessee became a fortnight off school. 'When I got back, they wanted to know where I'd been. And my mother just wouldn't lie. If she'd told them that I'd broken my leg everything would've been all right. But they said I had to do all these detentions, which I always had a shitload of anyway; I was getting

punished for telling the truth so I just went 'well, screw you'. That was a lousy attitude to have, but it pissed me off.'

He dropped out of school immediately, a move he regrets. 'It's always been a problem for me, not having enough education to get along.'

He didn't manage so bad, though. Early in 1968, playing under the name The Warlocks, Dusty and Rocky ran into Frank Beard - like them a native of Dallas, like Dusty a high school drop out.

Frank worked days as assistant manager in the sports department of the International Super Store, selling fishing rods. Nights were spent in the Fort Worth Cellar, playing drums behind a stripper. The group was called The Cellar Dwellers - another of Frank's teenage bands was The Hustlers - and in 1968 they were picked up by local entrepreneurs Wayne and Bob Steffek to record a single for the duo's own Steffek label. Both sides, 'Bad Day' and 'Call', were written by Tooty Tander and Randy Palmer, and the whole affair was forgotten almost as quickly as it was over. The Dwellers remained in their cellar and Frank found himself in the enviable position '...where I could do some wild things when I was in the mood to do wild things.'

Most of his wildness revolved around his

friendship with Dusty and Rocky Hill, a friendship which began with dropping acid and playing with The Warlocks, and continued with dropping more acid and dying his hair blue.

The Warlocks cut two singles under their own name, but their greatest moment came when they hitched up with an English singer, Lady Wilde. Backing her, The Warlocks could regularly be found playing Dallas cinemas, opening for British Invasion movies like *Ferry Across The Mersey*, *Hard Day's Night* and *Catch Us If You Can*. They made another single, too, again behind Lady Wilde.

But things were still lagging some way behind Dusty's dreams. Along with brother Rocky, Dusty - then aged just 14 - had played onstage behind the likes of Freddie King and Lightnin' Hopkins ('The guy who booked Rocky also booked people like that. And as they never had a regular band, we used to stand in. I learned very fast - through fear. Fear's a great teacher!' Dusty has since admitted). Downtown theatres and Lady Wilde were a step back for Dusty.

The Warlocks only made the one single with Lady Wilde. When she moved on the stage was set for Dusty, Frank and Rocky to put together a band closer to their own hearts. American Blues was born.

The bottom line was that American Blues were a pop band. Right from the start, their eyes were focused towards commercial acceptance, and the first step was to record a remarkably faithful version of the Tim Hardin classic 'If I Had A Hammer' for the local Karma label. It was, after all, almost five years since that song had last appeared in the American hit parade, but sadly, American Blues' version was not to change that. Its reception did, however, inspire the group to record an album and, appreciating the import-

Right: Dusty in the ring.
Below: Dusty Hill.

BARRY PLUMMER

ance of establishing themselves with an easily recognisable image, dye their hair blue to match their name.

'We just figured we could play more clubs if we had something going for us. But it was dyed blue, and we couldn't wash it out to walk around the street,' Dusty later admitted.

Frank, who bleached his hair seventeen times before he could get the blue dye to stick, remembers '...walking around downtown Houston like that. And back then, Houston was the murder capital of the world! I still shudder when I hear someone say 'Hey! Music man!' That's how we always used to get called out.

'Whether it was the album or the image that did it, no-one is sure, but American Blues swiftly landed themselves a genuine record deal with the Uni label. It wasn't a particularly major deal - the band cut just one more album - but it served to get them out of the Cellar, where backing 'female entertainers' with such numbers as their showstopping 'Chocolate Ego' and, when the acid was good, the Mothers of Invention's 'Freak

Out' album, supplying the group with the bulk of the beer and cigs money.

It was at the Cellar where American Blues first encountered Billy Gibbons - or at least, Lanier Greig who was, at that time, calling himself Billy Gibbons. According to legend - and one thing that must constantly be kept in mind is that much of ZZ's early history is confined to hearsay and legend alone - Lanier introduced himself to American Blues and suggested sitting in on a jam session.

Impressed by Gibbons' local reputation, the band agreed - then stood back in horror as Houston's so-called number one guitarist proved unable to even tune his borrowed instrument! Lanier, of course, had barely picked up a guitar

Above: Frank Beard.
Right: Frank Beard.

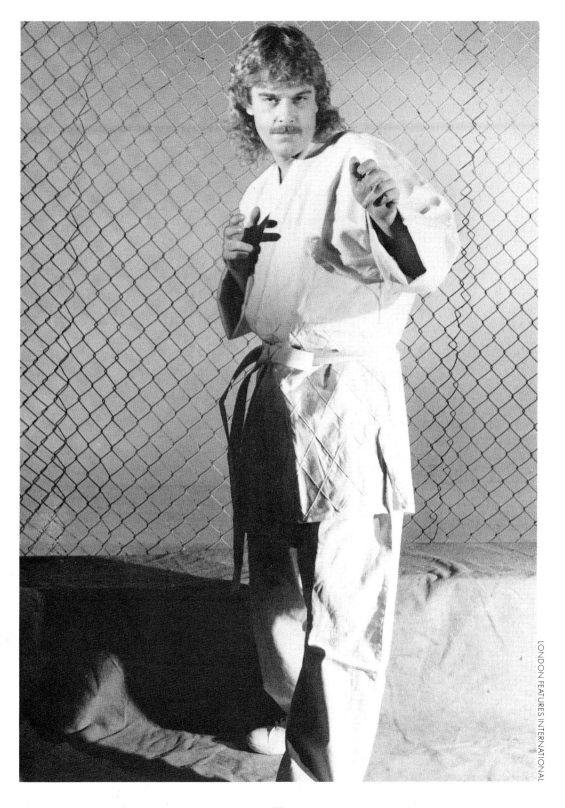

DAVID REDFERN

BARRY PLUMMER

in his entire life!

Billy's reaction to this remains unrecorded. Perhaps he considered returning the favour and introducing himself to American Blues as Lanier Greig, keyboard player par excellence. Or maybe he was simply too busy with some of his other enterprises. It was not, for instance, unknown for Billy to don priestly garb and set himself up as a door-to-door salesman, offering rubber 'Prayer Balls'. You throw them against the wall while you're praying and your prayers would all be answered.'

Or else he'd wrangle air-time on a local radio station and, posing as a minister, would '...feature the most hideous blues you've ever heard, real low-down nasty stuff. I wouldn't say it was done as a joke, but it was something a little different from the mainstream Bible bashers...'

And Billy still had his mainstream musical ambitions to settle. A year or so earlier The Moving Sidewalks had encountered Bill Ham, a local pop crooner-cum-promo man. No-one seems certain quite how they met. Billy claims it was at a Doors gig which The Moving Sidewalks were opening; other sources remember Ham

spotting the group when they accompanied John Mayall during one of his solo tours. Either way, Ham was an acquaintance worth cultivating. Having got his musical career out of his system after releasing one, totally ignored, single for the Dot label, Ham moved into promotion, first with Dot, but more recently with Daily Record Distributors in Houston.

Bill Ham's real ambition was to do a Colonel Tom Parker. To pick up an unknown act and mould them into the biggest thing to hit the United States since Kentucky Fried Chicken. Sunshine Tucker, a receptionist at Daily Records who once worked for Parker, proved an invaluable source of information as Ham plotted his masterplan.

First off, he wanted a blues band - a real blues band - dirty, unshaven, the smellier the better. He even had the sleeve of their first album planned. It would be called 'Back Down In The Alley', and depict his hobo heroes sprawling amid garbage cans in Salvation Army cast-offs.

Billy, Dan and Lanier heard him out with growing enthusiasm, even contributing to the madness with a suitably obscure, blues-ey name

BARRY PLUMMER

for the group: ZZ Top.

Above: Dusty.

'The name is our secret, and remains eternal,' Billy told *Record Mirror* thirteen years later. 'The one thing I can tell you is that it has nothing to do with Zig Zag or Top cigarette rolling papers. 'Out goes one theory. Another, similarly dismissed, is that bluesman Zo Zo Hills entered into their calculations somewhere. Whatever the truth behind the name, it was indisputably the sole property of Messrs. Mitchell, Greig and Gibbons, and someone, somewhere, has the registration slip from Paris County Courthouse to prove it.

Opting not to augment their line-up with any further musicians, the three-piece ZZ Top lost no time in making their first single. It was recorded at the quaintly named Robin Hood Brian studio in Tyler, Texas, and financed by Daily Record Distributors, and two growling blues numbers, 'Salt Lick' and 'Miller's Farm', were laid down. Both songs were group compositions which duly appeared on Bill Ham's specially founded Scat label. Distribution, of course, was through the Daily organisation.

Things were not stable within the ZZ Top camp however. Only weeks after recording 'Salt Lick',

Lanier Greig was invited up to New York by songwriter Jeff Barry (of Ellie Greenwich, Phil Spector and Shadown Morton fame) to audition for a part in 'The Cowboys', a Monkees-style TV comedy which Barry was casting. Greig, of course, went; by the time he returned to Texas Billy had sacked him. And after all that, 'The Cowboys' failed to take off. From there on Lanier dropped out of circulation, reappearing only once - in 1979 - as synth player on an album by 1994.

Lanier was replaced in ZZ Top by Billy Ethridge, a one time member of The Chessmen. But no sooner was he installed in the group than Dan Mitchell was out on his ear. He walked into a band rehearsal one day to find the two Billys jamming with Frank Beard, an old friend of Ethridge's. Doubtless, Billy G. tried to convince Dan that Frank's appearance meant nothing, but

neither party was under any illusions as to Dan's continued role in ZZ Top. Dan followed Lanier Greig into limbo - and not too long afterwards was joined there by Billy Ethridge, pushed out of ZZ Top to make way for Frank's old crony Dusty Hill.

Billy told *Melody Maker:* 'I met Frank through a fellow in Dallas and he came down and after one show he said he'd got a drummer who I had to meet. That was Frank and we teamed up there and then. Then the guy from Dallas Billy Ethridge quit so I needed a bass player, and Frank knew Dusty, and that's how he came to join us. I didn't know it, but Frank and Dusty had worked together for about five years before.'

'The first time I ever heard Billy play was when I played with him,' Dusty said. 'We did a shuffle in C and it lasted 45 minutes. One song. It was good, y'know.'

Early ZZ Top sessions, like those of The Moving Sidewalks, The Coachmen and The Saints before them, took place at Billy's house. Father Fred did his best to ignore the din; apparently his favourite method of relaxation was to sit reading sheet music in the way other people read magazines. But the band certainly knew how to rouse him. A musical perfectionist, it only needed one bum note to emerge from the garage for Fred to rush in and scream, 'That was meant to be a C Sharp you idiot!'

'I remember Billy's dad coming into rehearsals and sayin' 'No guys, that's wrong,' and you just didn't argue with him because he was so knowledgeable about music,' Dusty told the *New Musical Express.*

'Freddy was the only person I've ever known to change the entire air conditioning in his house because it was a half-tone out of tune with his piano,' added Frank.

'Salt Lick', ZZ Top's first single, was fairly successful around Houston, at least in as much as it brought the group to the attention of the promoter responsible for putting together a tour of blues legends at the start of 1970. Muddy Waters, Howlin' Wolf and Lightnin' Hopkins topped the bill; ZZ Top were to open the show. It wasn't until they turned up for the first date that the promoter realised he had booked a *white*

act, the only one on the tour. If ZZ Top had ever wondered just how authentic their attempts at the blues were, they now needed no further evidence. Even the tour's audiences, exclusively black, gave the group a rousing reception.

'There was a poker game going on the whole time,' Frank told David Thomas of *You* magazine. 'These guys were wonderful - the best poker players I've seen. They'd get down in the dressing room, get out a Fender bass guitar case and pull it across their knees. Every one of them would get out a .45 and a wad of money. 'They'd be playing poker and somebody would come down and say: 'Muddy, you've gotta go onstage.' And he'd growl and say 'Don't anyone take my money'. He'd walk off and leave his dough and his gun. He'd do his set and then come back and just get right on with the game.'

Towards the end of the year ZZ Top set about recording their first album, again financed by Bill Ham's employers at Daily Records Distributors. Much of the material dated right back to the days of Dan Mitchell and Lanier Greig; several

Right: In the backwoods: 1973.

DECCA

sources have even suggested that both had a hand in the composition and were only dissuaded from pressing their claims by Bill Ham. Certainly it is true that Lanier had some sort of agreement with Ham and Gibbons. Even on the first single he remained uncredited, ostensibly because he was under contract to the Acuff-Rose publishing house and nobody wanted to pay them a percentage for using Lanier's talents.

'ZZ Top's First Album', as the set was called, was never particularly representative of the band's power. Despite the quality of such songs as 'Neighbour Neighbour' and 'Back Door Love Affair', the record was a jumbled mishmash which depicted nothing more than the sound of a band thrashing their way through some often frighteningly unfocused self-penned blues standards. As a producer Bill Ham was barely more proficient than Steve Ames, who had overseen The Moving Sidewalks, and it has been suggested - cruelly, but not inaccurately - that if Bill Ham's intention was to portray his protegés as a bunch of country boys who'd just stumbled out of the moonshine shed, he succeeded beyond his wildest expectations.

'In this day of homogenized rock, synthesized music, retakes, over dubbing, multi multi-tracking, an honest recording by accomplished musicians is a rewarding pleasure,' claimed the album's anonymous sleeve notes. 'ZZ Top's First Album is just such a recording. This is the way blues rock is meant to be played: openly, honestly and spontaneously. It takes an experienced, sensitive group like ZZ Top to capture the *abstract blues* from within and combine it with the ability to feel and play good hard rock

without losing their communication. 'An introduction to the band? Or an excuse for the ragged rawness of the record? ZZ, alone, know the answer to that one.

During the recording of 'ZZ Top's First Album', Bill Ham and the Daily brothers began negotiating with London records. 'I told London I'd got 'em the next Rolling Stones,' Bill later said, smiling slyly at the way he touched a very sore point with the record company. After eight years of togetherness, the Rolling Stones' contract with London (Decca in the United Kingdom) had just lapsed, and the Stones had no intention whatsoever of resigning. They went off to the massive Atlantic stable, leaving London with nothing more than back catalogue reissue rights and an obscene paean to male prostitution, 'Cocksucker Blues', in lieu of a final contracted single.

London took Ham's bait - at a price. They needed assurances from both Ham and the Daily brothers that not only would *they* be responsible for financing studio time, but that ZZ were guaranteed to sell enough records in Texas for there to be no danger of London losing any money at all. They, London, would cover the costs of mastering, pressing and distributing the album. That was all.

Infuriated, but aware that he'd be lucky to get any better offers, Bill Ham accepted London's deal - much to the glee of Billy Gibbons. He told *Rolling Stone*: 'As long as I could remember I'd played those Rolling Stones records and wanted to have my own band on that label.'

The day London repressed 'Salt Lick' and released it as their first ZZ Top single, that ambition had been achieved.

CHAPTER 3

Waiting for the Bus

True to Bill Ham's word, London Records found themselves with a best seller in the Lone Star state. But throughout the rest of the country - nothing. And that was despite Ham putting the band on tour for as many as 300 shows in that first year. There was one period where they played 210 shows without once going home. They'd get home for Christmas, of course, but tours just ran into one another without a break. If there was a support spot vacant, chances were ZZ Top would fill it, especially in Texas where they opened for everyone from Alice Cooper to Peter Frampton and back again.

'We were big in Texas,' Dusty later lamented, 'but at that time, most people thought Texas was really hick, and a band from Texas was a hick band. A lot of people thought we were a country band!'

And yet the deep South, at the dawn of the 1970s, was one of the most potent breeding areas in American rock. The West and East coasts might have had their own indigenous scenes and gathered press interest because of it, but throughout the South - in Texas, in Arkansas, in Alabama, in Georgia - home grown rock was rising with a vengeance. Fiercely provincial, and seemingly intent on providing nothing beyond a backlash to all those years when the South had been synonymous with country and western, white rockers had until now been forced to emigrate east or west to ply their trade. Now a new breed of shitkickers was attempting to return rock 'n' roll to its spiritual homeland.

The Allman Brothers, from Macon, Georgia, the leading lights of the Capricorn label, were the first to break through: two albums and as many years of relentless live work established them far

beyond the boundaries of Georgia. In their wake came the Marshall Tucker Band, Grinderswitch (formed by the Allman's roadies and best known in Britain for supplying the theme music for the seminal John Peel Show), Area Code 615 (whose 'Stone Fox Chase' was similarly utilised by the British *Old Grey Whistle Test*), Edgar and Johnny Winter, Wet Willie, and from Florida, Lynyrd Skynyrd, whose anthemic 'Free Bird' was a maudlin tribute to the late Duane Allman which climaxed in a volley of screeching guitar lines and ascended into the pantheon of rock classics within moments of the band being wiped out when their private plane crashed in the Mississippi backwoods in 1977. And then there was Black Oak Arkansas, a sprawling seven-piece who had no time for the niceties of the Allmans *et al*, but spent their entire career locked in that frozen moment when a country hoedown turns into a Bacchanalian orgy.

It was as part of this illustrious company that ZZ Top launched their own assult on the hearts and minds of middle America, barnstorming their way from club to dive and spending their time off

in recording studios, working out their next record. There was a masterplan, of course; no band in their right mind could ever consign themselves to an eternity of touring without having at least one eye on the potential rewards. But if ZZ Top were planning to annex the other forty-nine states of the Union, they were going about it in a quite idiosyncratic manner. They were Texas boys and proud of it. Their heritage oozed out of every pore, out of every song. They sang like cowboys, they dressed like cowboys. And if they didn't exactly play like cowboys that was only because they had been prepared to open their ears to music other than the bar room balladeering which made up the schedules of their local radio. In years to come in 'Heard It On The X', they were to sing the praises of the 'X', an outlaw radio station set up by Doc Brinkley back in 1936, just across the border from Del Rio, Texas.

Brinkley had been based in Missouri, but had been banned from the airwaves by the communications watchdog, the FCC, for selling goat gland sex operations to farmers. 'And he made a fortune,' Billy told *You*. 'Guys came from all over the country. He finally got his broadcasting licence revoked, so he went to the Mexican authorities, who were just thrilled that he was down there. He built a five hundred thousand watt monster station just eleven miles across the Rio Grande and it was just blasting out across the United States...

'It not only covered the U.S. and Canada, but also beamed south to Antarctica, East and West Indies, and parts of Europe.

'During the Second World War the Germans came over and tried to take the gear back to Europe with them to use as broadcasting equipment, because they couldn't buy it there. There was a big shoot-out down there, but they lost.'

Billy and Frank, even today, take great pleasure in recounting tales of Brinkley's exploits.

Right: Waiting For The Bus.
Below: Dusty & Billy: the Red Guitars from Texas.

Playing country and western to attract farmers, he enlarged on his original stock of goat glands to sell chickens, harmonica lessons, hillbilly and gospel records - 'They even had autographed prayer cloths of Jesus Christ!'

Brinkley also won the services of seminal DJ Wolfman Jack, and with him came a diet of blues and rock 'n' roll. *Rolling Stone's* John Morthland gave the following account of Jack, and his activities in 1981. 'He played only the finest blues and spent the night howling at the moon between (and during) records, advising listeners to 'get yo'self nekkid' and dig the music, all the while peddling various snake oils, plastic replicas of Jesus, coffins and inspirational literature. He was assumed to be black, but wasn't; he kept his secret by refusing interviews and public appearances...until the Seventies.'

It was these roots which ZZ Top assimilated and then regurgitated on the road. And the view from the road was sufficient to give them a fresh perspective on what they were trying to do, the imagery which they wanted to recreate. It gelled with 'Rio Grande Mud', ZZ Top's second album.

Again financed by the Daily brothers (an arrangement which was to last through to the recording of ZZ's next record), 'Rio Grande Mud' saw ZZ Top labouring under no misapprehensions about the critical response to their strivings. 'ZZ Top's First Album' had been almost unanimously savaged by the press, and while the group needed to point to nothing more than that peculiar brand of provincial prejudice which has forever divided northern critics from southern musicians, they were still hurt by the criticism.

'I'm so sensitive to all that stuff,' Billy was to say five years later. 'Most creative people are. I guess to have your thing panned like that has got to result in some kind of adjustment. 'And adjustment was exactly what 'Rio Grande Mud' served up.

It was *not* a particularly eclectic album; ZZ Top still ploughed a solid groove through their beloved blues 'n' boogie, but they relaxed a little in their self-consciousness. 'Rio Grande Mud' was not so slavishly devoted to establishing the band as bona fide bluesmen; instead it set out to depict a hard rockin', hard workin' rock 'n' roll

REX FEATURES

Above left: "Okay, where'd ya put that razor smartass?"
Above: "A to E, right?" Billy & Dusty on stage.

band. The songs still overflowed with Texan imagery, that strange brew of Confederate chauvinism and Latino sloppiness.

Nowhere was this so evident as in 'Francine', a song co-written by Steve Perron and Kenny Corday, and deservedly recognised by all concerned as the most commercial thing on the entire album. Released as a single, 'Francine' was sung in English on one side of the 45, and Spanish on the other.

Perron and Corday had both been members of The Children at the time 'Francine' was written, and even then Billy had set his heart on recording a version of the song. His ambition was furthered the night he sat in for the injured Cordray at a Children gig in Houston.

For ZZ 's version of the song, Billy claimed a co-writing credit, although most observers believe he did little to the song beyond make a few structural changes and alter Steve Perron's original 'If I catch her with Billy G' line to 'If I catch her with Stevie P.'

It was this line, obscure to anybody bar those 'in the know' as it was, which provided problems for the translators employed to write a lyric sheet for the Japanese release of 'Rio Grande Mud'. Not being aware of the true nature of a 'Stevie P.', they replaced the unfortunate Perron's name with some exotic imagery of their own. There were no such problems for the Mexican bar band Dusty stumbled upon one evening. They played the English version of the song, but when Dusty introduced himself and congratulated the band on their version, the Mexicans responded blankly. They'd learned the song phonetically, from the radio - obviously Billy's decision to record a version of the song in *their* native language had fallen on deaf ears. Nonetheless, 'Francine' still gave ZZ Top their first ever chart success, coming to rest at number 81 in a

with ZZ Top, Pearly appears on the cover of 'ZZ Top's First Album'. She was also such a staple part of Billy's recording armoury that the first time he recorded a song with a different guitar, he titled it 'Apologies To Pearly'.

There's a story behind his ownership of Pearly of course. A girlfriend, an aspiring movie actress, sold her 1930's Packard during a trip to Los Angeles. With the proceeds, she mailed Billy four hundred and fifty dollars - exactly the amount he needed to buy the guitar from an old farmer who'd been keeping it under his bed.

No-one seems to know just what Billy was doing, ferreting around beneath strange farmer's beds like that, but Texan rock 'n' roll folklore is awash with tales of similar finds. During the 1940's and 1950's, the age of Bob Wills and Woody Guthrie, every other cowpoke in the county owned a guitar. It was part of their tradition, picking out 'Home On The Range', 'Streets Of Laredo', *et al*, but when the tradition went into retirement, so did the guitars. Many are the tales of young would-be rock 'n' rollers who, working from old bundles of sales receipts and warranties lifted from the back rooms of neighbourhood music stores, would spend their time wandering from farm to farm in search of long discarded

Cashbox Top 100 then dominated by the soft, sweet soul sounds of The Chi-Lites and Roberta Flack, the Metallic sludge of Grand Funk Railroad and Steppenwolf, and the MOR whimsey of Neil Diamond and Harry Nilsson.

'Rio Grande Mud' was a remarkable album; remarkable not only for the proficiency of the material it contained, but also for the wealth of legends which have grown up around its best loved tracks. 'Just Got Paid', for instance, drew such an enthusiastic reaction from the audience that the band was forced to withdraw it from the live set for fear of being hurt by the loose change which showered the stage whenever it was performed. 'We had to make the decision whether the fifty dollars or so we picked up from playing that song was worth all the bruises,' Billy said later. But he admitted that it was a song which simply begged some sort of reaction. Dusty told *Rolling Stone*: 'I have this friend I grew up with. He works in a factory, he's got two kids, a working man, you know. And our song 'Just Got Paid', he and his friends *love* it. Every pay day they go to this beer joint, have a few and they play the song over and over.'

And then there's 'Apologies To Pearly'. Pearly Gates is the 1959 sunburst Les Paul guitar which, Billy told *Rolling Stone*'s Kurt Loder, makes ZZ Top sound like 'four flat tyres on a muddy road'.

Too valuable to make public appearances

LONDON FEATURES INTERNATIONAL

antique axes. And a find like the Pearly was priceless. No wonder Billy was sensitive about hurting the old girl's feelings!

'Rio Grande Mud', while it didn't have much effect against the barrier of Northern prejudice which damned its predecessor, was still a sizeable success around the South. But locally established as they were, life on the road for ZZ Top was still to have its ups and downs. The ups were nights like the one when they played alongside Chuck Berry, 42-years-old and still playing guitar like he was a-ringin' a bell, and were paid five hundred bucks for the privilege. The downs were places like the National Guard armoury in Alvin, Texas. They drew one (1) paying customer.

Dusty picks up the story: 'We figured we were there so we might as well play for him. So we did four sets and between sets we'd go out and talk to him, buy the kid a coke.'

Such gestures characterised not only ZZ Top but a whole breed of American bands from the early 1970's whose modus operandi was the non-stop tour. ZZ Top's own ongoing affair with life on the road has already been mentioned, but

equally devoted to carving their way across the continent were bands like Kiss, Grand Funk, Foghat, Aerosmith and myriad other, less commercially significant, outfits. For the first time in years, at least since the arrival of The Beatles, record company hype counted for nothing in the rock market-place — or very little, anyway. RCA could pour as much money into breaking David Bowie as they wanted, but it wasn't until he took his 'Diamond Dogs' tour around the States that he was rewarded with anything greater than a cult following. Conversely, Casablanca could exist on a virtual shoestring but make it look as if the next decade's business lunches rode on Kiss' gaudily painted shoulders, at the same time allowing the band's larger than life appearance work its spell over the masses.

It was into this category that ZZ Top fell. Not

Below left: Zap! Pow! Pedal!
Below: Customised rocker covers and air filters.

that London was penniless; they owned the back catalogue of the Greatest Rock 'n' Roll Band In The World and in the three years following the Stones' departure put together almost as many posthumous compilations as the band left behind in official albums. But their investment in ZZ Top had not exactly been generous. It is said that when Bill Ham offered ZZ Top to London, he asked for ten thousand dollars. London gave him a tenth of that. And while the band showed a profit from both live and vinyl work, so much money was ploughed back into the group that occasions such as the night ZZ played the New Orleans Warehouse and ended up sleeping on the stage after the gig were by no means rare occurrences.

But, as Billy says, it was worth it. Holding back on some expenses made other investments possible, and if there was ever a turning point, a moment where ZZ Top could stop suffering the

blues and start simply playing them, it was the day they broke open the piggy banks and splashed out on a pair of Marshall Super Lead amplification stacks. 'We got them, Model 1959s, and just went wild. They were so beautiful!' he enthused.

The secrets of ZZ Top's sound are multitudinous. The Marshalls are certainly part of it, whether displayed at face value or disguised beneath the band's private label Rio Grande face plates. So, claims Billy, are the .008 gauge Lone Star Slims guitar strings which he sells for $7 a set through the ZZ Top fan club and which are supposedly made from melted down car fenders. Then, of course, there's his use of a peso instead of a plectrum. But the stacks were the turning point, and even today, all the way across America, there are people who can tell you about the day that li'l ol' boogie band from Texas came to their town - and blew the place away.

CHAPTER 4

Hot Blues and Righteous

On January 21, 1973, The Rolling Stones opened the second leg of a world tour at the International Sports Centre in Honolulu. They played two nights on Hawaii and from there it was off to Hong Kong, New Zealand and Australia. The support band, in Hawaii at any rate, was ZZ Top.

'Bill Ham set it all up with Concerts West,' Dusty said. 'We went onstage and people just looked at us, dropped their jaws and moaned: 'They're a *cowboy* band!' In the end, though, we'd just blow them away and they'd scream for us to come back. We'd feel kinda funny with the Stones watching us from behind, waiting for *us* to finish.'

The Stones shows kicked the year off in fine style. The release of ZZ Top's third album, 'Tres Hombres', would see it out even finer.

For the first time, ZZ decided to try working in a different studio. They settled for Ardent, in Memphis (although they did some work at Robin Hood Brians) and with one-time Led Zeppelin engineer Terry Manning helping Bill Ham out behind the scenes, ZZ Top turned in an album which many aficionados still regard as their finest *ever*.

'Tres Hombres' was hard, direct and brutal. From the rip-roaring punch of the opening 'Waiting For A Bus' through to the closing bar-room squalor of 'Have You Heard', it was a magnificent album. *Kerrang!* magazine described it as 'one of the most awesome hard rock albums ever recorded'; the American public deemed it worthy of two million bucks worth of sales. And as 'Tres Hombres' made its way up

the chart, so 'La Grange', the band's latest single, rocketed skywards and gave ZZ Top their *Cashbox* Top 30 debut.

'La Grange' owed its origins to field trips which Billy had taken during ZZ's earliest years. Aware that Texas had so much to see if only you took the trouble to find it, he would drive relentlessly up and down the state, stopping at greasy roadside bars and grills, downtown clubs and upstate brothels. 'La Grange' was one such brothel; Gracie's Chicken Farm was its real name. In later years it would again be immortalised in the Dolly Parton/Burt Reynolds movie, *The Best Little Whorehouse In Texas*.

The establishment was a hundred years old by the time it was closed down - closed, Billy claims, after being '...exposed by an over-zealous reporter after a touch of notoriety.'

'The real sheriff was seventy years old,' Frank told *Sounds*. 'He didn't look like Burt Reynolds. The reporter in the film didn't look like the real reporter either. I play golf with him...'

'La Grange' won a spot of notoriety as well; as it climbed the chart, rumour had it that Canned Heat were contemplating suing ZZ Top for plagiarising their 'Fried Hockey Boogie' riff - a claim which was patently ridiculous. The Stones' 'Shake Your Hips' was always the song's role

model; that, and the Slim Harpo riff from which the Stones had originally pinched the notes.

The success of 'Tres Hombres' should have relieved ZZ Top of much of their work-load. It brought in more money than the trio had ever seen before, and if it didn't quite allow Billy to indulge in another of his more outlandish fantasies - to buy an entire shopping mall - the royalty cheques at least meant he could open an expense account at a few of the shops.

But far from slackening off and enjoying their new found wealth, ZZ Top threw themselves into a touring schedule which was exhausting even to think about. Sleeping in the bus, or on friends' living room floors, they took every booking they could. They knew they'd arrived; now they had to ensure they stayed. One night, not untypical, they were booked into a tiny township in the wilds of Michigan. 'We had three days off before the gig and when we got there it was terrible,' says Dusty. 'It had one movie house, no nightlife and the water smelled like sulphur. We pulled into town and said 'What's happening?' They said 'ZZ Top are here in two days'. That was it! We were the only excitement!'

Another occasion illustrates the tight finances under which the ZZ ship sailed. 'We were in Lubbock, staying in this hotel opposite the venue', says Dusty. 'Our equipment didn't turn up and we had to cancel the gig - and we couldn't even

afford our hotel room! We were all sharing one room; one had the bed, one had the mattress, one had the pillow and the blanket. We had to sneak out of the hotel. We were hanging out the window on a rope!'

And if things were like that in the South, the area where ZZ fever was at its highest, imagine what life was like when ZZ crossed the Mason-Dixon line and ventured up the East Coast! Talking to *Rolling Stone's* Gordon Fletcher, Billy admitted that the territorial ups and downs of ZZ Top's career were fast becoming an obsession with the band. An obsession which could only be assuaged by a complete breakthrough. 'It's just a matter of exposure,' he said. 'People have got to hear us before we can hope to sell them our records.'

'It's no accident that they're this big in the South,' Bill Ham told Fletcher. 'When we were just getting started we must have played a couple of hundred gigs a year, all of them in and around Texas. We played so much that word-of-mouth started carrying our reputation and that's the way it's gonna have to be up North, too.'

There were plenty of barriers to break down, though. As *Rolling Stone* pointed out, the Northern market looked on ZZ as 'little more than a Southern Grand Funk'; an appellation which might not have bitten so deep had ZZ merely had critical disfavour to contend with. But while Grand Funk sold millions with their every release, at the time of the *Rolling Stone* interview, 'Tres Hombres' had still to top 300,000 copies. After forty weeks in the record stores, it had yet to breach the magical Top 50 (Gordon Fletcher spoke of the album 'surging to number 59 on Billboard's chart').

But the ease with which the South had fallen did instil some confidence into the band. Regarding touring Dusty was to say: 'Hell, if we didn't want to play in front of people, we wouldn't be much of a band would we?', while Ham,

Right: Tres Hombres: 1973 in Nudie suits.

having hustled his way on to the same stage as Uriah Heep, Mott The Hoople and Alice Cooper (whose 1973 outing was then one of the biggest grossing in rock history), regarded the saturation of the East and West Coasts as little different from the subjugation of the South.

ZZ even took to emphasising their provinciality, describing themselves as 'that li'l ol' boogie band from Texas', and appearing on stage resplendent in flamboyant, brocaded Nudie suits. Now they could look like cowboys and sound like them.

Ten gallon hats, sequined rodeo jackets, spurs and knee length Cowboy boots; 'The Nudie look was fine because it was so far gone it was back again,' Billy laughed later. 'But I went off that look when John Travolta's *Urban Cowboy* thing happened in America (a 1980 James Bridges movie which, with its Texas rodeo scenarios, catapulted cowpoke chic to the height of fashion). The look became so fashionable it was vulgar!'

'My idea was for ZZ to become a people's band,' Ham said. 'We played a lot of out-of-the-way places, playing for the people at people's prices. It's harder that way, and takes longer, but once the band has established itself as a

DECCA

people's band, the people won't leave you.' A later *Rolling Stone* piece likened Ham's words to those of Jimmy Carter's Presidential speech. Substitute the word 'music' for 'politics' or 'government' and the word 'concert' for 'primary' and you get a fair idea of the intensity of Ham's long crusade: '*(This) will be the year when we give the music of this country back to the people of this country. This year we have had thirty concerts, more than ever before, making it possible to take our campaign directly to the people of America... This has been a long and personal campaign, a rumbling experience, reminding us that ultimate music influence rests not with the power brokers, but with the people.*

'That is to say, the people's right to boogie to a people's band shall not be denied, regardless of regional origin.'

The contradictions of ZZ Top's standing were many. In Houston, for instance, they were able to headline a massive festival, appearing onstage in front of a rapturous crowd who, in LA or New York, would already have had their money's worth from supports Wishbone Ash, Savoy

Brown and The Doobie Brothers. In New Orleans, the Warehouse was so oversubscribed when ZZ appeared there that club owner Bill Johnston announced that he could have sold the place out for five more days. And on Independence Day 1974, they played the Texas Memorial Stadium in Austin, urged on by 80,000 rabid fans who loved nothing so much as the fact that local heroes ZZ bill-topped over Joe Cocker, Santana and Bad Company.

But up in New York - as *Melody Maker's* Chris Charlesworth pointed out in May '75 - ZZ Top couldn't even half-fill the 5,000 seater Felt Forum, and not even Bill Ham's remark that most New Yorkers had fled the city for the Memorial Day holiday could dampen the story. 'It seemed like every show we did, somehow, something would go wrong. Either it'd be a state holiday, or something would go wrong mysteriously during our set. We came up at a weird time, while a lot of the top acts were kinda going down a little bit...'

Above: On stage, 1984

RETNA

ROSS HALFIN/REPFOTO LONDON

LONDON FEATURES INTERNATIONAL

Above: Mushmouth shouting.
Left: Blue jean jacket blues: Billy, 1984.
Above right: The Eliminator.
Below right: Goin' Down to Mexico.

BARRY PLUMMER

ROSS HALFIN/REPFOTO LONDON

LONDON FEATURES INTERNATIONAL

LONDON FEATURES INTERNATIONAL

Unspoken was the accusation of foul play, of headlining roadies and musicians 'accidentally' pulling the plugs on these upstart cowboys who were usurping them in front of their own audience. Because ZZ Top never respected anybody. You could be the biggest band in the world, but if ZZ were on your bill, you better watch out!'

'In the old days the pressure was on us because nobody knew who we were and we had to play the best we could, just so people would remember us,' Dusty said. 'Then later, we were better known, but the pressure was still on us, because we had to prove we'd been worth remembering.'

And they were worth remembering. ZZ Top's career, if plotted on a graph, would be a continual upward line, never dipping, never levelling. From playing to one person in Alvin, to eighty thousand in Austin, ZZ's rise was nothing short of meteoric. And Bill Ham, perhaps poring over just such a chart, knew that the peak would soon be in sight. 'Tres Hombres' became one of the biggest selling albums of 1974, in America at least. Other bands, like the Stones ('It's Only Rock 'n' Roll'), Paul McCartney ('Band On The Run'), Grand Funk ('We're An American Band') and Elton John ('Caribou') might have scored more memorable chart toppers, at least in the eyes of critics, but nobody could denigrate ZZ Top's achievement.

And it wasn't only records which they shifted by the truckload. London Records revealed that almost half of the band's sales were accounted for by cassette and 8-track tapes. Billy told *Rolling Stone*: 'The finest compliment I ever got was in South Carolina. This guy walks up and says 'Hey man, I wanna tell you I really dig your tape.' I said 'What?' He said 'Yeah, I dig your tape.' He didn't say record, he said *tape*. He said

Right: Snappy Kakkie Balinese style.

ROSS HALFIN/REPFOTO LONDON

Above: Billy with the Texas axe.
Far right: Have you heard? Billy in the UK, 1983.

RETNA

'Man, me and my chick really dig getting into the back seat with your *tape*.'

'It is such a reward for me to go to the beach and find ZZ in every van, in every station wagon. ZZ is such a tape band! God!'

The reasoning behind this was simple. ZZ play fast and hard. They have drive. They move straight ahead. When you're racing the car ahead you don't want Genesis or Pink Floyd or any other closet intellectuals recycling their public school playing field fantasies. You want music which matches your mood, music which celebrates the open road in the windshield and open legs on the back seat. Driving along to ZZ Top don't make you cerebral, but it *can* make you horny.

All that remained now was for ZZ to set about consolidating their initial success, to pull out an album which would not only establish them within rock 'n' roll's hierarchy, but would put an end to all the cowboy-boogie orientated sniping which so satisfied the band's detractors.

The late Lester Bangs, for five years an editor of *Creem*, for ten a contributor to *Rolling Stone*,

ranked high amongst these detractors. Discussing Heavy Metal in the latter magazine, he wrote ZZ Top off in a line, labelling them a Boogie Band, summing up their raison d'etre as 'the eternal reiteration of simple riffs for the sake of 'partying'.... They wear cowboy hats,' he concluded scornfully.

Bangs later became a convert to the ZZ cause himself; in the meantime, his was the voice of a whole subsection of America's rock marketplace who say, and perhaps feared, in ZZ's frenzied simplicity, the direct antithesis of all that rock had come to represent in the mid-1970s. No matter that he championed The Stooges, Mott The Hoople, The New York Dolls, Bangs, and others like him, believed in rock as a weapon. For social change, for political change, it didn't matter. It had to serve a function, and even the most nihilistic excesses of the most drug crazed garage band could fit the bill if you were prepared to dig deep enough. But bands like ZZ Top, like Cactus and Black Oak Arkansas, for them things were simple. They had no great message for the world, they had no revolutionary rhetoric. They

LONDON FEATURES INTERNATIONAL

could, if one was so inclined, be likened to some great musical steamroller, heedlessly bludgeoning everything which stood between it and the 'Rawk 'n' rawl paaarty!', the pot of gold at the end of their personal rainbows. Small wonder that ZZ Top had no time for critics. For a long time, they refused even to do interviews, reasoning that if the press didn't like them in concert or on vinyl, they were no more likely to like them in person.

They did, eventually, relent on this score, but with a perversity which could only have grown out of their distrust of the media. They made a point of insisting that interrogators did *not* record the conversation. 'We don't wanna be misquoted,' Billy would growl, waving aside the logical rejoinder that misquotation was far more likely if the hapless scribe was left to rely purely on note taking or, even worse, memory.

Tactics such as this (and it remains true to this day, enshrined even in the pages of *The Book Of Rock Lists* under the heading of the ten least promising interview openers - no. 6: 'We don't believe in tape recorders') were unlikely to endear the band to those who make their living from reporting the lives and times of rock 'n' roll. That may even have been the intention. The press didn't like ZZ Top; ZZ Top didn't like the press. But both knew that they needed each other; the press knew ZZ could help them sell papers, ZZ knew the press could help them sell records. The tape recorder ban was just another skirmish in an ongoing war of nerves. Now it was time to wheel on the really big guns.

'Fandango' was the album which was to finally establish ZZ Top as a power in the land. Half live, half studio, it recaptured intact all the power and glory of ZZ's live show. 'This music is brought to you honestly, without the assistance of studio gimmickry,' claimed Bill Ham's liner note. And it was. What could be more honest than the sound of a rock 'n' roll band going down a storm

Below: Three Wise Men.

BARRY PLUMMER

LONDON FEATURES INTERNATIONAL

Left: "No, you put your finger here".

REX FEATURES

in front of one of their regular packed houses at the New Orleans Warehouse? Or that same band going hell-for-leather in a tiny upstate studio, playing live there as well, capturing every-thing in just one, occasionally two, takes and throwing overdubs, multi-tracks and 'so on out the window.

'Fandango' was still an unusual move in that most live albums are Greatest Hits - or at least, greatest *bits* - packages. But a brief 'Jailhouse Rock' and a faithful retread of Willie Dixon's 'Mellow Down Easy' aside, all the material was new. But it wasn't the songs that mattered. What counted was the atmosphere, the energy, the sense and strength of purpose which oozed from the record's grooves and proved once and for all that here was a band you could *trust*. There was no hype about ZZ Top, no bullshit. 'Fandango' was, as its sleeve promised, hot and spon-taneous. There was no artificial flavouring in ZZ Top. Just as Lester Bangs had always said, they were committed to just two things - beer drinkin' and hell raisin'. And you can intellectualise all you want, but when you get to the bottom line, that's what rock 'n' roll has always been about. 'Fandango' sold a million.

CHAPTER 5

Beer Drinkin' and Hell Raisin'

On August 16, 1975, the *Billboard* Top 40 finally opened up to ZZ Top. 'Francine' came close, eighteen months before, peaking at number 41 and only just missing out on the hallowed playlists of the nation's AM radio shows. But now came 'Tush', a song so lewd, so crude, so ridiculously sublime that it immediately fell into the repertoire of virtually every bar band in the country. Half a decade later it even won the Hollywood seal of approval when John Belushi sang it in *Old Boyfriends*. It also accompanied a bar-room brawl in *An Officer And A Gentleman.*

Yet even this success was no easy ride. 'The word 'Tush' has some very finely defined meanings in the United States, and few of them correspond with Billy's claim that the title was originally lifted from 'Tush Hog', an old Roy Head B-side. Most of them, in fact, refer to a certain part of the female anatomy. 'In Dallas,' Billy claims, 'Tush, means 'plush'. Something fine. So it could mean what you think back East, but it could also mean what we think down here. There again, it could mean both things, like that's a tush tush.'

He elaborated no further, and despite its Top 40 rating, many radio stations banned the song on grounds of obscenity. 'It's just a song about going out and looking for somebody,' Dusty has explained. 'Everybody does it.'

And judging by the record's reception, almost everybody likes to go out and buy records about it. 'Tush' cracked the Top 20 and would undoubtedly have risen even further had it not been for those idiot radio bans which made sure that a good proportion of ZZ's potential audience never even got to hear the song. Probably just as

well, though. 'Tush' would have been a strange bedfellow for The Eagles, The Bee Gees and Van McCoy's 'Hustle' in the balmy days of August, 1975.

'Tush' happened in its entirety in one take at a soundcheck,' Frank said. 'We started playing this riff, and the way it was written is exactly the way we played it that day. That was easy. It's not like beating your head against a wall writing.

'When we go in we don't want to play our own material, and we'll start doing something totally off the wall, and that's where a lot of the original ideas come from. Especially when you're road weary. You come up with some weird ideas...'

'We're relaxed when we're recording,' Dusty says. 'Even when we did 'Fandango', the studio side of it, up in Tyler, which is totally dry. There's not a drop of alcohol to be had in the entire place! There are things about the studio which are enjoyable, even though we are basically a working live band. You have the freedom to put something down and erase it and put something else down instead. On stage you play and

RETNA

that's it.'

Billy said: 'We're still learning about a studio and we're anxious to learn. But it's a time consuming process, so we're still concentrating on what we know best.'

What ZZ Top knew best was the live show. They'd proven that with 'Fandango', and they'd proven it with the string of attendance records which now seemed to exist solely for ZZ to top. On June 9, 1974, they smashed Elvis Presley's record at the Nashville State Fairgrounds. On September 23, 1974, the Rolling Stones' Long Beach Arena record fell. On July 3, 1975, they went to Tulsa and outdrew local lad Leon Russell, and on July 26, 1975, ZZ replaced the mighty Led Zeppelin as the most popular band ever to play the New Orleans City Park Stadium. But if those statistics were impressive, they were nothing compared to what ZZ Top had up their sleeves next.

More than a year elapsed between the release of 'Fandango' and ZZ's next album, a year in which the group, far from ploughing their all into producing a second slice of definitive Texas boogie, instead opted to diversify a little. 'Tejas' was an album of mixed styles, ranging from the deranged rock 'n' roll of 'Arrested For Driving While Blind' to the mellow acoustic beauty of 'Asleep In The Desert', through to what

BARRY PLUMMER

Frank described as the 'disco-reggae' of 'Snappy Kakkie'.

In March '76 ZZ rented a warehouse for a home base while they rehearsed for their next tour. According to Billy: 'We hired a room and made some noise in it for three months. Basically it was just garnering ideas we had put together on the road from the previous tour. ' He told *Sounds:* 'We were in the room grinding away every day. We were staying over there for eight, ten hours a day. We knocked out about four tunes, then went up to the studio to cut them.'

From there, the trio headed off to the Ardent studio in Memphis where, with house engineer Terry Manning at the controls, they began to explore the same strain of mutant disco which had so inspired The Rolling Stones during the making of their 'Black And Blue' album. Again, Billy told *Sounds:* 'Inevitably, in most forms, there will be someone to surface who can handle it (disco music) well, and lately it's been refined to

RETNA

ROSS HALFIN/REPFOTO LONDON

the point where it's really become quite interesting, in terms of the latest sounds. I've taken a liking to it, and we've tried to get into the groove a little bit.'

Not that ZZ Top were likely to be cracking open the dance charts for a while yet. Their forte, their trademark and their reputation, still revolved around beer drinkin' and hell raisin', and if 'Tejas' as a whole indicated that the band was not afraid to open up and embrace other areas once in a while, 'Arrested For Driving While Blind' proved nothing if not that ZZ Top were happiest when laying down the fiercest three-chord rumble they could lay their hands on. Pulled off the album as a single, 'Arrested... ' gave ZZ Top their fourth hit single, albeit peaking at a lowly number 74 in the *Cashbox* chart.

'That song, I guess it's a hold over from those old Chuck Berry days. You know, I read recently that Texas features seventy thousand miles of toll-free highways,' Billy said. 'That's how I've seen Texas, it's got to have an impression to write about.'

'Tejas' overflowed with that imagery. 'Pan American Highway Blues' was about just that; a road which stretches all the way down through Mexico, Central and South America. 'Balinese' dealt with the Avalon Highway, a 'little old spot we knew about. I don't want to say resort, that sounds too high class. And this place was a real dump, it had gambling, girls. Oh, it was a wild place, out in the sticks. ' And then there was 'Asleep In The Desert', based on the time Billy and girlfriend Micky found themselves stranded without gas in the middle of the desert.

'We'd been camping up outside of L.A. with some friends of ours, so we just picked up our sleeping bags and hiked a mile or two into the desert and stayed there the night.

'There's an old saying about the desert part of Texas that says: 'If you get lost, don't worry. You'll have plenty of company. The vultures'll visit you by day, the coyotes will visit you by night, and the red ants'll keep you company.'

Elsewhere on the album, Billy tried his hand at playing country fiddle, a 1941 Rickenbacker elec-

tric which he'd had '...lying around for a long time. I brought it out on the road and just started horsing around, so we decided to use it on 'She's A Heartbreaker'.'

Almost inevitably, 'Tejas' turned platinum, and just to compound their status as one of America's top rock attractions, ZZ Top now turned their attention to a tour which has gone down in the annals of history as one of the biggest, the baddest and the best ever.

The mid-seventies had seen some of rock's biggest guns wheel out their most ambitious and expensive road shows yet. David Bowie, The Rolling Stones, Kiss, and Alice Cooper had all set out in a spirit of totally over-the-top one-upmanship, all hell bent on smashing each other's attendance records and sending tallies set by The Beatles over like ninepins. ZZ Top vanquished them all. Six months long, the Worldwide Texas Tour was nothing short of a phenomenon. According to *Newsweek*, it saw ZZ shift more records at the height of the outing than even the Stones had during their 1975 jaunt. 1.2 million

RETNA

people witnessed the show, eleven million dollars was grossed from ticket sales alone, and it took one thousand, four hundred and forty man hours simply to erect and dismantle the stage. It was, in terms of equipment, the largest show ever taken on tour; even the trailers used to haul the gear around were part of the show, painted with Texan panoramas. The portable stage, shaped like Texas, measured three thousand square feet and weighed thirty five tons. The rest of the gear accounted for another forty tons. The sound system pumped out a skull shaking forty thousand watts.

And then there were the animals. A hundred and forty thousand dollars worth of native Texan wildlife - a longhorn steer and a buffalo who rose up on either side of the stage on Sizzor lifts to bask in white spotlights for fiteen seconds. Five tethered buzzards. A couple of rattlesnakes. A wolf. Cacti and corrals completed the illusion. Also on board was a havelina pig - a band mascot who would hang out in the dressing room or wander around the backstage bar looking for free drinks. And finally, the A.S.P.C.A., popping up at various points en route to ensure that the beasts weren't being ill treated.

They weren't. Ralph Fisher, a rodeo clown who was in charge of the animals, took every possible precaution to ensure that the creatures were comfortable. The rattlesnakes had their own plexi-glass dome, fully air conditioned, set in the Brownsville section of the stage. For weeks before the tour, he played ZZ's records to the menagerie to acclimatise them for their stage debuts. And such was the ease with which the animals settled down, by the time *Rolling Stone* caught up with the outing, in New Orleans, the buzzards were content to sit on their fence and prune their feathers, while the wolf had grown so accustomed to his fame that, instead of opening the show with his scheduled howling, he sat on the edge of the stage and tried to shake hands with the photographers and road crew. In the end he was replaced with a tape recording.

The rattlesnakes didn't fare quite so happily. Overly sensitive to vibrations as they are, the poor things grew increasingly agitated as the show progressed, and long before the tour was out, they, too, had had to be removed.

'This whole thing could have crippled us,' Bill Ham admitted. 'But I have a great respect for people who love music and I think they appre-

RETNA

ciate taste and that's what I've tried to do here; to take a little Texas culture to people who've never seen a buffalo. I think audiences appreciate you if you do something extra. Smoke bombs, laser beams? All that's been done so many times.'

Nevertheless he confessed that the whole enterprise could have fallen flat on its face. 'I can't afford to make mistakes,' he told *Rolling Stone's* Chet Flippo. 'If you have an act as big as ZZ Top, you *better* make the right moves.'

The tour had, he claimed, been planned as painstakingly as any Presidential campaign. It had taken a year out of his life, selecting venues, sending key advance men ahead to gauge local response, stroking the radio stations. 'And it came off. Six months on the road, playing every venue large enough to accommodate the entourage, performing on average once every three days - that was the minimum time needed to erect, dismantle and transport everything. ZZ took the expectations of a continent and turned

them on their head. Bands like Kiss could boast of putting on an extravaganza the likes of which had never been seen in a rock arena before, but their silly masks and costumes, levitating drum kits and rocket firing guitars were little more than a space age update of those old Busby Berkeley musicals. ZZ Top took the whole idea of a rock show further than anybody ever dreamed, and their only regret, the band said, was that they had been unable to take Texas to the rest of the world.

Talking to *Sounds* in February, 1977, Billy had tentatively promised that ZZ and co. would be hitting the United Kingdom and Europe some time in the spring. Six years later, he revealed that the main stumbling block, and one that ultimately proved insurmountable, was the continent's quarantine regulations. As it was, ZZ Top weren't to reach Britain until 1980; and a lot of water would flow under the bridge before then.

Lowdown in the Street

By the time the Worldwide Texas tour came off the road, ZZ Top had been on the road almost without a break for six years. The Moving Sidewalks, American Blues and so on added another four or five years to that tally. That made eleven years of cramped hotel rooms, broken down vans and greasy roadside cafe food. If ever a band deserved a holiday, it was ZZ Top.

Yet, few groups would have even dreamed of taking a break at this stage in their career. Two platinum albums were still selling around the country as recent converts sought out vinyl souvenirs of the Texas tour. The Yankees had finally succumbed to the Confederates; if ZZ wanted to play New York, they only had to look at a venue for it to sell out. They'd breached the Top 20 singles chart. The world, or at least the United States, was at their feet. But ZZ Top wanted a holiday, and a holiday is what they took. A three year one.

Today, of course, there's nothing unusual in a band taking a break like that. Even in 1977 it wasn't unknown - Emerson, Lake and Palmer once waited a full thirty-six months between albums, Pink Floyd took nearly as long. More recently, groups like Fleetwood Mac released new records only when the shine had finally left their last platinum mega-monster. John Lennon even waited five years before following up his last record. But folk like that can afford to hang about. No-one doubts their superstar status; some people think they even keep people waiting deliberately, knowing that the expectations of the fans can only be heightened by the delay.

ZZ Top, however, were *not* in that position. Sure they were big, but so were a lot of other people. Sure they had platinum albums and sell-out tours. So did Kiss, so did Black Oak, so did K.C. And The Sunshine Band. And you wouldn't catch *them* throwing it all to the wind and rushing off to Nepal, Paris and all points obscure.

'We didn't break up,' Frank says in answer to suggestions to that effect. 'We just needed a break. When it happened we had no idea how long it would last.'

Frank took advantage of the lay-off to 'get straight'. Tales of his capacity for drink and drugs are numerous - even Frank admits that he was 'a black belt in drugs.' He had problems, and he wasn't scared to face up to them.

'I was irresponsible and self centred,' he says, 'just like all young self-serving dope fiends are. It was me first and to hell with the rest of it.'

His favourite poison, he says, was smack. 'The heroin would be serious, to the extent that when I was in Houston I was able to maintain a habit. When I was on the road it was more diffi-cult. You can't maintain a habit because you can't carry enough, unless you're Keith Richard.'

He denies that his playing suffered. 'I never lost my primary talents, just all my secondary

talents. Like being able to brush my teeth.'

Frank checked in to the Palmer Drug Abuse Program in Houston, an institution with which, after he came out clean, he maintained links. Recently he sponsored Carrie Hamilton, daughter of actress Carole Burnett, when she was involved in the programme.

Sadly, Frank's second wife (his first marriage, when he was 15, had ended in divorce, and Frank spent several years being served with subpoenas for child maintenance every time ZZ played) didn't pull through. But once rehabilitated, he married for the third time, settling down with Debbie, a girl he knew from way back when, when she'd been married to Neil Ford and The Fanatics' drummer. She, too, was married

twice before meeting Frank.

Dusty Hill's vacation was spent wandering around Mexican villages which, he told *Record* magazine, he likes to frequent 'when things get too heavy.' He laughed off suggestions that he spent his time in a fat farm, pointing to Billy and Frank as the sources of *that* scurrilous rumour. It was, apparently, a long standing band joke that when Dusty could not be found, one or other of his colleagues would remark: 'Oh, he's making

Below: Slip, gully and cover point: MCC Top.

LONDON FEATURES INTERNATIONAL

himself scarce because he's afraid Bill Ham wants to send him to the fat farm.'

It was Billy Gibbons, though, whose 'What I did on my summer vacation' essays have come in for the most reiteration. He told the *New Musical Express:* 'I had joined the Board of Trustees at the Contemporary Arts Museum in Houston through some associates of Dusty's brother (Rocky) and this group of artful sinners from Houston, and we all became quite close hanging around. And there was an announcement of an unveiling in Paris on some antique musical instruments that had been found in some monastery in India. We were invited to watch, and two of us from Houston went, and they had the opening of these boxes of musical instruments which was fairly interesting.

'Then this French girl says they are going to Nepal to look for more instruments, and did we want to go. So we said 'Sure!' We got there and found we had to trek for fourteen days.'

Of course, with Billy heading off to Tibet, the Abominable Snowman had to make some kind of appearance. The hunt for exotic musical instruments became a 200 mile search for the Yeti, and Billy - true to form - came home with the news that: 'I had an encounter with something up there. I don't know what it was, but I wrote a song about it, called '(I Wouldn't Touch It With A) Ten Foot Pole'.

'What was happening in Paris was finding new ways of making art out of inexpensive mediums,' Billy says. 'Polaroid, Xerox, and they were all legit. There was some nice stuff being done. This was right in '77, '78, and Xerox art became a *bona fide* piece of the punk scene. What we were doing musically was more uninspired. Just synthesized environmental music, it was like air. Trying to rip off Brian Eno. It was fun.'

While his protegés were off pursuing their private fancies, Bill Ham worked on their public career. Gone they might have been, but ZZ Top were not forgotten. And Bill knew that, happy as the London label was with their lil'l ol' boogie band from Texas, there were plenty of labels who would be even happier. And who would be a lot more willing to pay for them than London had been. The going price was one million dollars,

RETNA

and in September 1978 he got it. ZZ Top signed to Warner Brothers.

The band immediately began work on their next, sixth, studio album, but in the meantime, Warners bought up the rights to ZZ's past records from London. The logic behind the move was plain. Back at the beginning of the decade, after The Rolling Stones quit the company (coincidentally for Atlantic, one of Warners' sister companies), their back catalogue had remained at their old company's West 25th Street offices where it was recycled with what often seemed quite malicious regularity. The sheer productivity of London's (and, in England, Decca's) repackaging department has already been commented upon; that in itself was not over remarkable. It was the timing of these releases which so offended. In March 1971 the Stones released their first Atlantic album 'Sticky Fingers'. In April, Decca put out the 'Stone Age' compilation. The following January, with the release date of the Stone's 'Exile on Main Street' set getting closer every day, London unleashed 'Hot Rocks And

Fazed Cookies', a greatest hits package, *and* the England only 'Milestones' set. In 1973, the Stones' own 'Goat's Head Soup' was countered by the rehash 'No Stone Unturned'; in 1975, when Atlantic released their own 'Best of...' compilation, Decca retaliated with a collection of *unreleased* material, and to add insult to injury, scheduled it to hit the shops on the same day as the 'official' compilation.

It was an absurd situation for any band to be in, and Bill Ham must have had one eye on the Stones' predicament when he gave Warners the go-ahead to buy up ZZ's own back catalogue.

London Records had, in fact, already taken some steps towards getting maximum mileage out of the goldmine which ZZ Top bequeathed them, although - in fairness - they did it while the band was still under contract to them. In 1977, with ZZ's own plans - and whereabouts! - unknown, they pieced together 'The Best of ZZ Top', a surprisingly imaginative hotchpotch of cuts from the band's six albums to date. There were a few unforgiveable omissions of course: 'Arrested For Driving While Blind' seemed a particularly foolish absentee, especially as it only just slipped from the Top 100 when the album arrived. Also from 'Tejas', 'It's Only Love' surely merited inclusion as well, again by virtue of its chart-cracking exploits (despite only reaching number 46, it had remained on the *Cashbox* chart for

fourteen weeks; less than 'La Grange', but a month longer than 'Tush', ZZ's biggest hit to date).

Long term ZZ watchers were disappointed, too, by London's failure to include any of the cuts which remain tantalisingly unavailable on album; 'Salt Lick', 'Miller's Farm', the Spanish language version of 'Francine'...any of these would have been more than welcome.

No matter; the anonymous compiler won at least a few friends with his selection of 'Backdoor Love Affair' (from 'ZZ Top's First Album'), 'Waiting For The Bus' (from their third) and - best of all - the brooding 'Blue Jean Blues', the best song Elmore James never wrote and Peter Green's Fleetwood Mac never recorded.

Green, the brilliant young guitarist who single-handedly powered Mac to peaks which no other British blues band have ever scaled so successfully, has never received less than the highest praise from Billy Gibbons. He's up there with Hendrix and Clapton, to the extent that Billy was to tell the *New Musical Express*: 'When we got together, the American bands were playing a style of music that didn't seem to have the excitement that a lot of the English bands had, particularly on the (John) Mayall records with Clapton and then Peter Green and all that stuff, which was so heavily blues influenced and yet wasn't laid back. They'd picked it up where it left off before it died here, and I think that's what drew us towards that.'

In another interview with the same paper, he said: 'What I could never understand is how the American bands have such a weird interpretation of the blues compared to the English bands. We gravitated towards the English sounds, the way English guys were playing the blues, because they didn't have the notes too high, they had nice vibrato, excellent tones. We wanted to play a technically acceptable kind of music rather than what a lot of American bands were doing to the blues - like Quicksilver and that sound.'

Or, as Dusty growled: 'Once you learn the fourth chord you're out of the blues.'

ZZ Top paid their own tribute to the spirit of the English bluesmen when they tackled Elmore James' 'Dust My Broom' on their next album

64

'Deguello'. Fleetwood Mac's version is probably best known today, but the song was, of course, essentially an American experience. James himself was born in Mississippi, but didn't record until 1952 - just eleven years before his death. 'Dust My Broom' was his first hit; subsequent reissues ensured that it was his last hit, too, but in the interim he put his name, and distinctive style of guitar playing, to a host of songs which today form the staple for any self-respecting blues diet: '12 Year Old Boy', 'The Sky Is Crying' and 'Look On Yonder's Wall'.

The other cover version on 'Deguello' was 'I Thank You', an Isaac Hayes number. It was fiercely sexual, both in terms of the band's delivery and Billy's treatment of the lyrics. Simply by changing the original word 'Me' to 'It', he completely restructured the song. 'You didn't have to hold it, you didn't have to squeeze it,' he sang.

Despite such innuendoes, when 'I Thank You' appeared as a single in March, 1980, it lost little time in racing into the *Billboard* and *Cashbox* Top 50s. Its eventual peak of 34 in the former

listing gave ZZ only their second ever AM radio smash.

The album's finest moments, though, were songs like 'Cheap Sunglasses', 'Manic Mechanic' (about a seven foot tall racing driver Billy once knew - or so he says) and, best of all, 'I'm Bad, I'm Nationwide', the song which, at long last, saw ZZ's blues and humour finally integrated into one stupendous whole.

So 'Deguello' was a great album; no surprises there. But there were a few new ingredients in the band's potent brew. 'Hif-Fi Mama' and 'She Loves My Automobile' both saw the debut of The Lone Wolf Horns, sneaked into the studio while producer Bill Ham's back was turned, and left for all the world to hear on the two tracks where the Lone Wolves' self-confessedly inexpert honking could cause least offence. According to Billy, the Lone Wolves had but one saxophone lesson each; according to the sleeve credits Dusty (tenor), Frank (alto) and Billy (baritone) weren't any more accomplished themselves.

'Trends dictate instrumentation to a degree, unfortunately. The Stones were forerunners in

RETNA

using saxophones when the very word was absurd,' Billy says, confessing that ZZ's use of the instruments was their 'trying to capture that black spirit, exploring the hard R&B thing.'

Frank explained: 'We wrote 'Hi Fi Mama' and we said if ever a song needed horns it's this song. We've never used any outside help before on any of our records (untrue! Pete Tickle, ZZ's road manager, played acoustic guitar on the second album). Like Billy will get down on this knees and play an organ's foot pedals with his hands or something. We've always managed to get what we wanted ourselves. And so I said, 'Let's go buy saxes and learn how to play saxes. It can't be that hard.' So, we did. We went and we plopped the money down for three of the finest saxophones made and hired us this musician in

ROSS HALFIN

Houston that plays saxophone to give us lessons. We learned each scale and Billy wrote the parts out because he could transpose.

'Billy'd say 'You blow this and you blow this and I'll blow this,' and we'd blow these three notes and they'd sound pretty good, so okay, that's the note. We just went through and figured it out. I think we each had about twelve notes that we had to play through the whole song. We learned that and then we practised and practised. I think we spent two hours a day for a month just running the tape of that song and playing parts with it until we thought we had it and took it into the studio and did it. Ahh...it was so fine. We made a whole production of it.'

He told *Modern Drummer*: 'I'd love to be able to play the saxophone and I still honk on it. I can make some of the world's ungodliest sounds come out of that thing. But it's so frustrating when you're proficient on one thing and try to start on another that's so totally different.'

The success of 'Deguello' was such that Warner Brothers almost instantaneously recouped their initial investment. Yet when the record first appeared, the critical resistance to it, and to ZZ themselves, was as strong as ever. In some corners, at least.

'Just in case it has escaped their notice, America has undergone one or two mighty big changes in the years ZZ Top have been away,' opened one review. 'Five years ago, people might - at a pinch - have tolerated these mean lookin' hombres and their woolly west-via-Las Vegas supperclub blues mongerings. My granpappy even reckons they had a couple of million sellers back then as well. But the times, they've been a-changing. ZZ Top last recorded in 1976, and no doubt back then, they did seem a little subversive, a little dangerous. But since then, we've had the Pistols, we've had The Clash and

DAVID REDFERN

we've had The Ramones. And try as I might, I can't find a single thing on *this* record ('Deguello') which makes me sorry for that. It's out of date, out of time and, as soon as I finish writing this and get down to the exchange shop, it's out of my house.'

The inference, of course, was obvious. The end of the 1970's had seen a whole new movement erupt from the gutters of the cities and into the hearts and minds of an entire generation. Distilled as it might have been by the time it hit America, the shock waves of Punk Rock still reverberated round the heart of the industry; the East and West Coast centres had turned nihilism (or a vague approximation thereof) into a national pastime. But what the self-ordained prophets of punk failed to realise, sequestered as they were at the very epicentre of its effect on American rock, was that while *their* lives might have been irrevocably altered by Rotten, Strummer and Costello, there were vast tracts of their continent where beer guzzling party minded adolescents cared nothing for the niceties of the New Wave, and still liked nothing more than to carry on wallowing in the same old excesses as they always had. That was why Kiss records sold in platinum truckloads while the Pistols were canned off in Fort Worth. New York and Los Angeles might have been America's head and heart, but all points between would remain faithful to those who were faithful to them until the end of time. That was why 'Deguello' mattered

and why the inane ramblings of its detractors didn't. Maybe it's true that the public have a short memory. But treat them nice and they'll soon start remembering again.

With this in mind, it wasn't really surprising when Lester Bangs and Robert Christgau, two of rock's most demanding critics, and ardent ZZ haters to a man, executed a very neat *volte face* and actually came out in favour of 'Deguello'.

Christgau wrote: 'These guys got off the road for real...sounds as if they spent all three years playing the blues on their front porches. The strident arena technique (which marred earlier records) is gone, every song gives back a verbal phrase or two to make up for the musical ones it appropriates, and to vary the trio format, they've figured out where to put them. 'And then, in reference to the upsurge of similarly intentioned albums to emerge in the wake of John Belushi and Dan Aykroyd's *Blues Brothers* movie smash, 'I've heard a shitload of white blues albums.... This is the best by miles.'

Lester Bangs went so far as to put his new-found faith to the ultimate test. Said Dusty: 'Lester blindfold tested that album on his hard-core punker friends. And they dug it. The 'Cheap Sunglasses' thing, down the line it's been changing. I think the times have allowed our kind of music to be embraced by a wider range of people. I knew it when we played Miami and purple heads turned up. Mohawks, they're all there.'

CHAPTER 7

Snappy Kakkie

1980 saw ZZ Top make their long awaited return to gigging. And with it came a few more surprises. Out went the cowboy clobber. As Billy put it: 'It breaks my heart to see the ashes of *Urban Cowboy*-ism being dumped in Texas, and I'm just as much a proponent of the Cadillac with cow horns and ten gallon hats and a cold six pack as the next guy. But I just couldn't take it any more.' In came boiler suits, industrial boots and...beards. Long beards.

'In 1979 we got back together after the lay-off. I'd been to Nepal, Dusty'd been to Mexico and Frank'd been to the Caribbean. Me and Dusty discovered we'd grown fourteen inch chin blisters in that time,' Billy said. 'It was so ridiculous we just said 'Hey, we can have a lot of fun here', and they've stayed ever since. Frank just has the name beard. He'd shaved his off...'

When *New Musical Express*' Barney Hoskyns asked, 'Will you never grow a beard, Beard?' Frank replied: 'I can't! I'm just so far behind. I used to say I was too young, but after twelve years that stopped working. Then I said it was due to female thigh burn, but I got married and I can't say *that* no more. So now I just say I'm out of the race....'

The tour which unveiled the new look was to become ZZ's biggest grossing yet. And they achieved it without once having to wheel on buffalo and buzzards - a relief to Frank, if nobody else. 'It was hell working with those buzzards,' he later reminisced. 'If you stopped moving for a second they decided you were dinner and started pecking. I had to keep drumming the whole time and even then they'd still have a go.'

But the absence of such blatant visual stimuli in no way dampened ZZ Top's appeal. The outing earned them some of the best notices of their career, with extra special praise reserved for appearances by none other than The Lone Wolf Horns!

Said Frank: 'We made a film of us playing saxophones so, whenever we went on the road, we'd lower a screen and The Lone Wolf Horns would walk out and join us for three songs.'

The 1980 tour also saw, for the first time, ZZ Top hit Britain. They had only three UK dates - a TV appearance on the *Old Grey Whistle Test* on April 15, followed by two nights at London's Hammersmith Odeon a week later.

Billy was the only one of the trio to have visited London before. Back in 1969, an earnest young vegetarian on his way home from a few days transcendental meditation with the Maharishi in the mountains of northern Italy, he stopped over at Heathrow Airport, there to grimace his way through a genuine English steak and kidney pie.

Of ZZ Top's live appearances, he said: 'It's funny, because we waited so long to go to the UK, it was actually ten years before our first

REX FEATURES

Quo, boogie boys supreme, and good old Cream, themselves stranded in a kind of cultural no-man's-land by the retrospective realisation that truly they had been too bluesy for metal, but too loud to be anything else.

The connection, once made, however, was hard to argue with. Just as so many bands, in so many fields, before them had discovered, the British music scene thrives on convenient labelling. Instantaneously, therefore, ZZ's arrival in Britain, an event which should have been heralded from the roof tops, was instead passed over by all but a handful who didn't get their jollies from the then-prevalent ska/bluebeat boom which was sweeping the country. ZZ were, indeed, greeted by a 'nice little cult following'; two half-subscribed nights at one of London's premier venues and a smattering of warm reviews from critics already converted long before the band arrived.

The gigs at least stirred the British record buying public into a state of curiosity. 'El Loco',

appearance. Having found a nice little cult following, it was a very warm reception in the beginning, and yet so many things had changed in music. We were very uncertain about how a ZZ Top-type band would go down in the UK, especially since the wave of new stuff in the late seventies. We were lucky to hit it just as a heavy metal thing was coming back. There was a slot we could sneak into.'

The slot had been created by the emergence of what, claimed its acolytes, was the New Wave Of British Heavy Metal; bands like Iron Maiden, Saxon, Def Leppard, Ethal The Frog and a myriad more. But it was hard to see just how, or where, ZZ Top fitted in with the new metallic consciousness. Even at their most riff-sodden, ZZ had never offered more than a passing nod towards the merchants of metal; if Blighty had conjured up any equivalent to ZZ Top it lay in an unholy and purely hypothetical union between Status

Left: Arriving at Gatwick.

ZZ's next album, released in July 1981, made a brief appearance in the British chart - it came to rest at number 88, twenty-eight places below the band's only other UK hit, 1975's 'Fandango'.

If 'Deguello' had seen ZZ Top at last finding common ground between their love of the blues and their quirky sense of humour, 'El Loco' - their seventh LP - found them revelling in a new freedom of expression which that discovery allowed. Songs like 'Tube Snake Boogie' and the abominable showman's paean to the abominable snowman - 'Ten Foot Pole' - were truly funny and, in the case of 'Pearl Necklace', truly lewd ('Pearl Necklace' is Texan slang for fellatio).

'El Loco' was also the band's most eclectic collection since 'Tejas'. 'Heaven, Hell or Houston', described by *Kerrang's* Mick Wall as 'quintessentially evil', and a dead ringer for Blind Faith's 'Presence Of The Lord', was a *tour de force* of special effects, while the exquisite 'Leila' - 'ZZ Top's first and last ballad!' the band claim - was just that. Billy has described the song as ZZ's 'one chance to meet the Beach Boys', and only the most unfortunate bad luck could have pre-

vented the song from giving ZZ another well deserved hit. It peaked at number 76.

Most important of all the songs, though, was 'Groovy Little Hippy Pad', the first of a triumvirate of definitive ZZ songs (the others were 'Heaven, Hell Or Houston' and 'Party On The Patio') which closed side two. For the first time ever, ZZ recognised new technology; electronics and synthesizers were in evidence, and the result was one of the most commercial sounding songs ZZ Top had ever made. And the most unusual.

Frank told *Modern Drummer* how it came together: 'We built that song up at my house. We started out on the synthesizer, then built in all the other instruments piece by piece. That was a lot of fun, because the synthesizer is so relentless in its time keeping. I mean it's just perfect. It's just a clock going off. We did the whole thing a piece at a time. All of it was just layered in there.

'We did some strange things with 'Heaven, Hell Or Houston' (as well). We didn't know what we were going to do with that. We had this piece of a song, and we didn't have a bridge for it. So we just kept the bass drum going and counted off x amount of bars and then went back and decided 'Well, let's do something exotic.' Up at Ardent in Memphis they brought in this box of special percussion instruments and we tried all of them. We were beating on microphone stands, you know. I think we ended up with some temple bells in there, and an agogo. And trying not to play as though you were taught. Playing left handed or something like that to give it a little bit of a rough feel so it would sound more native.'

Prior to the release of 'El Loco' ZZ took another extended vacation - not too extended, it lasted a mere six or so months, enough time for them to recharge their batteries in readiness for the next American tour, and to sort out a new image.

The beards, of course, stayed, but now ZZ wore parachute suits. 'We got 'em in Colonel Bubby's Purveyors of Fine Surplus,' Dusty said. 'The Colonel had three left that he'd put on the rack at a high price. He was waiting for three fools to walk in.

'Trouble was, those suits were already old when we got 'em. By the end of the tour we'd

sewn them up so many times that they'd fallen apart. Plus, they smelled bad. Yuk!'

Billy told *Kerrang!*: 'What we wanted to do was find the sort of futuristic outfits used by Stanley Kubrick in the movie *A Clockwork Orange*. But y'know, it's difficult to find such similar things in America, so we ended up with the best substitute.'

'Actually, it was more *Clockwork Apple*,' Frank snorts. 'They refused to wear the black codpieces!'

The 'El Loco' tour was a success; the album was too. But *not* by ZZ standards. Although gigs still sold out well in advance of show-day, there was, it seemed, a distinct slackening off of fervour on the part of the audience. And 'El Loco' had only gone gold, a sobering reminder to the band that, as they approached their thirtieth birthdays all apart from Dusty who, Pete Tickle delighted in joking to visiting journalists, was pushing 48, so did their audience. And, at such a crucial crossroads in their lives, not every ZZ fan maintained the same priorities as they had at 25. The fact was, ZZ still appealed largely to the same audi-

ence as they'd appealed to all along. They weren't making new fans and that, as any band will tell you, is just as important, if not more so, as hanging on to the ones you've already got.' Only by meeting new blood could ZZ expect to inject new blood into themselves. Their very position in the music industry was precarious, and as the last encores of the last 'El Loco' show died away, the realisation must have been that for ZZ Top, make or break time had truly arrived.

Not that the band was likely to admit that things looked rocky. Sure Frank might still complain that it would be nice if ZZ could get a gold single, just to break the monotony of being known primarily as an albums-band, but beyond that, ZZ was still as crazy as ever. The stories of their humour, particularly Billy's humour, are almost as numerous as the sacks of mail which arrived at ZZ HQ after Billy sent out two thousand postcards, stamped with Dusty's name and address, in response to advertisements in sundry biker magazines. There was the time Billy wrote to NASA to ask if ZZ could be booked to be the first rock 'n' roll band to play the Space Shuttle.

And the gig in Florida, where Billy arranged for free records and posters to be given to anybody turning up on the night with free tickets from the Grand Caymans.

And then there was ZZ's penchant for hot-rods. As Dusty remarked, rock 'n' roll and hot-rods have always been synonymous; ever since the Beach Boys began cruising up and down Sunset Strip in souped-up T-Birds that couldn't be beat, ever since Jan and Dean took to wiping themselves out on Dead Man's Curve. Live fast, die young, and if you can go out in an auto pile-up, all the better. It's a tradition which can be traced all the way back to James Dean, Eddie Cochran and 'Tell Laura I Love Her'.

'We've always been car freaks,' Billy told the *New Musical Express*. 'A guy came into Houston and recommended we go with him to California for the National Drag Racing Championship, and not having been to one in a while, I really wasn't prepared for the magnitude and dynamics of a 2500 hp nitro-burning *bomb*. It was just like a rocket on wheels, it was so *awesome*. If there was a way to get that sound or that feeling on stage or record, well...'

ZZ's passion for drag-racing first manifested itself with the *El Dorado Bar,* a 1965 Chevrolet Impala convertible.

'A low rider. We had one, the ZZ Top low rider. A '65 Chevy convertible and they loved us. It had those lifts. *Low Rider* magazine did a feature on ZZ Top! Bob Merlis (the head of publicity at Warner Brothers) called me and said 'How d'you swing this?' I said: 'Bob? got a low rider?' He said 'You can't. A white man cannot buy his way into that magazine.' I think it was because I had one of the Imperials (a street gang) from East L.A. instal the hydraulic system in the car. The Imperials are badass, man. They are *the* low riders to deal with,' Billy said proudly.

Billy's dream car first began to take shape in his mind back in 1975. Browsing in a car showroom he discovered the famous *California Kid,* a customised 1934 Coupe, and a superstar amongst automobiles. The sight sent him rushing to Don Thelan's Buffalo Motor Cars company in Paramount, an eight-man operation which was itself spawned out of one man's dream. At the

BARRY PLUMMER

age of 14 Thelan picked up a 1940 Ford coupe for 35 dollars, pulled it to pieces then rebuilt it simply because 'it seemed a good idea at the time.'

Since then he's lived, breathed and worked hot-rods. In July '83, *Custom Car* magazine claimed he'd ended up '...with Buffalo, a shop full of cars, an Oakland winner, credits on many more, and by his own admission, spending more time on the phone than he does on cars. But that's business.'

'The guy who built the car is a bit of a racing nut,' Billy succinctly remarks.

The original plan was to build an almost exact replica of Pete Chapouri's *California Kid,* but Billy - and Don - always had far too much taste to simply copy somebody else's idea. After all, as one critic put it, 'It's OK to nick other people's tunes, but their cars? Cars are *personal*.'

The task of dreaming up the perfect motor went to Thom Taylor, Larry Wood and Kenny Youngblood, three of America's top custom designers. Their drawings incorporated everything *they* had always wanted to see in a car, plus everything Billy had wanted as well - almost everything, anyway. His plan of using gold records in place of hub caps fell through.

From the drawing board the car went into production. *Custom Car* examined the 'shopping list' in some detail: 'At the top (of the list) was a '33 Ford 3-window Coupe body, and second was a full Pete and Jake chassis to put under it. Hence the running gear follows a formula. At the front you'll find a SuperBell tube axle with transverse spring, tube shocks, four bar radius rods and Mustang disc brakes. And at the rear you'll find a nine-inch Ford live axle, again with a four bar, but this time with a pair of coilovers. The engine's a 350-inch Chevy, rebuilt with a mild cam, decent carb and manifolds and some milled ZZ Top rocker covers. The transmission is your basic Turbo 350, and the car steers thanks to a Vega box and a column out of a Chevy van. Underneath them, it's very much the basic American hot rod.'

Billy told *Record Mirror*: 'I suggested that Dan put a Corvette engine into it. What he didn't tell me was that the Corvette engine was used for drag racing. We were up to 140 mph and we got stopped for busting a radar trap.

'When the guy gave us the ticket he handed me the tablet to sign it and I kind of took it out of his view and changed the speed to 440 mph.

'I had to take this down to the DA's office and the judge was sitting there bored stiff with people running red lights and having no mufflers and stuff. This assistant DA said, 'I have you down here for 140mph'. So I just said, 'Your honour, there seems to be some discrepancy. My ticket says I was doing 440 mph and my car don't go that fast!' The police officer called me up afterwards and said, 'Gibbons, that was real droll!'

The mechanics of the car, of course, are fascinating themselves, but what really made the car stand out was the bodywork. Said *Custom Car*:

Above far right: The Heart Of the Beast.
Below right: Lowdown in the street.

BARRY PLUMMER

BARRY PLUMMER

BARRY PLUMMER

'Once they'd pulled it apart, filled the top and straightened out the doors, it went over to Steve Davis who fashioned the trick three-piece hood, and matched it into the grille. Then it was a case of finishing up the fenders, moving the headlamps lower down and nearer the grille, and finishing the deck lid and the rear pan which houses the licence plate.

'(Davis) put scoops into the hood sides... to emphasize them, make the body even swoopier and straighter and hopefully promote the ZZ Top aspect of the car. Youngblood did more drawings and in the end they agreed on the ZZ graphic in grey, yellow and maroon over the red body.'

And, of course, the car did drive. At fifty thousand dollars, it needed to. And although the band weren't into stock car racing, they decided to name Billy's beauty after the term usually applied to the fastest car in a race. Eliminator.

TEXAS ZZ
CHAPTER 8

Eliminator

ZZ Top's next album, 'Eliminator' by name and eliminator by nature, appeared in the spring of 1983. By August it had notched up sales in excess of six hundred thousand; when the corresponding tour hit Los Angeles, seventy thousand copies were sold in a week. 'It could so easily have failed,' Billy nevertheless insisted. 'We were trying to consciously broaden our appeal. But there was a magic about those recording sessions.'

Dusty told *Sounds*: 'It's a lot harder than 'El Loco',' agreeing with Billy when he said: 'We just hit on these heavier sounds. The heavier it got, the better we liked it. For one thing it's more fun to play live. We tried playing 'Leila' once and to hell with that. It feels better playing the harder stuff live.

'Also, we're having fun learning how to play the new stuff. We started off trying to do all of it in the set, but we're down to about five numbers now.'

'Eliminator' was a terrific album. Less conspicuously boogie orientated than its predecessors, it was still recognisable ZZ Top: Billy's patent 'four flat tyres on a muddy road' guitar sound was still at the front of the mix. But the sound was cleaner than before, less muddied, but without losing any of the band's characteristic density. There were some great pop tunes on there as well: 'Gimme All Your Lovin'', 'Sharp Dressed Man', 'Got Me Under Pressure' and, best of all, 'Legs'.

The synthesizers which made such an impact on 'Groovy Little Hippy Pad' made a welcome return to devastating effect. And that was despite Billy's admission that: 'None of us really knew

what we were doing with synths. It was literally a case of twiddling some knobs and hoping for the best.'

In another interview he claimed: 'We never had any qualms about bringing synths in, and it was strange because, although a few people said we had no business using synths, more people were saying we should have been using them more!

'But our fascination with them on 'Eliminator' was halted only by our inability to understand the machines; and the equipment, which in some cases was good for us because it minimised their use. We don't want to become a synthesizer band! And it's a great relief that we make an appearance and don't just rely on banks of synths. You know, ZZ Top won't be playing tonight, but their synthesizers will do it all for them! We still enjoy playing live!'

They needed to. The tour lasted eight months, closing in Biloxi on 12th February, 1984 (the band's fourteenth anniversary), and took in the whole of the United States as well as a sizeable jaunt around Europe.

The British dates began sporadically. On

August 20th, the group played the annual Heavy Metal festival at Castle Donington, sharing the bill with Whitesnake, Diamond Head, fellow Americans Twisted Sister and, making their live debut, Dio - the band formed by former Rainbow and Black Sabbath vocalist Ronnie James Dio. And all in front of what must be the most hard-core Metal audience in the world.

'It's odd. We didn't know much about the Donington festival,' Billy told the *New Musical Express* on the eve of the band's appearance. 'But ZZ Top fits the Heavy Metal bill in an Englishman's terms. And we couldn't be more ready to get into it with them. Maybe sometimes over here you have a tendency not to be so Metallish, but over there.... There's some bands in England that are so radical, what we do is light compared to a lot of it.'

Answering Richard Grabel's contention that maybe ZZ 'is just too American in its trappings to translate well across the Atlantic,' he continued: 'I don't know if the American-ness is a factor. What the Europeans can relate to is that we still hold trust in that original form of rock 'n' roll, which never really died in Europe. The big difference is that in the States, if it's old it's not good. However, Europeans tend to revere that which is good forever. We may not be fashionable in the techno-wave scene, but they regard our approach as valid.'

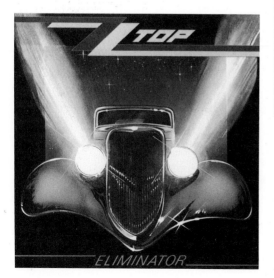

ELIMINATOR

ZZ returned to England in October for a one-off show at London's Marquee Club, treading the boards which, a decade earlier, had seen the likes of Cream, Fleetwood Mac and Jimi Hendrix when *they* took their first, historic steps into the world. The show was a highlight of Billy's year. 'It's been a very long time since we could go back and do a small gig like the Marquee, and we sure had a ball that evening,' he told *Kerrang!* 'Dusty and I had just taken delivery of our zebra striped guitars and there was certainly an air of great excitement and worry! I'm now a member of the club and I proudly show off my card to everyone as one of the nicest mementoes of the European tour.'

There again, a lot of ZZ's happiest reminiscences of Britain involve 'unusual' souvenirs. When they were over in 1980, Billy said, 'We were

ROBERT ELLIS/REPFOTO LONDON

in the elevator with two large Nigerian fellas. We had our white ZZ Tops on and they had on these embroidered African caps.

'When we reached the lobby we asked them what they'd take for the hats and they just looked down at ours. That's how we exchanged our ZZs for some Africanese.'

The tour proper began a month later, taking

ROBERT ELLIS/REPFOTO LONDON

DAVID REDFERN

ZZ through Leeds, Hanley, Manchester, New-castle, Glasgow, Birmingham and, finally, three nights in London; two at the Hammersmith Odeon and then, when ticket demand proved so high that the band could have filled out a conventional theatre six nights running and still have a sizeable lock-out, a triumphant showing at the giant Wembley Arena.

But ZZ were still appealing to either the converted or the merely curious. 'Eliminator' sold respectably in England, hovering around the lower reaches of the chart. Singles from the album - following the American pattern of 'Gimme All Your Lovin'', 'Sharp Dressed Man' and 'Legs' - garnered favourable responses as well. But if there was any one moment when ZZ Top could truly be said to have exploded out of the semi-cult secrecy which, even after the tour, was still their lot in the UK, it was the night *Rock Around The Clock* screened three consecutive 'Eliminator' videos.

The concept of ZZ even making videos in the first place was a strange one. Their *Old Grey*

Whistle Test appearance in 1977 was not only their first ever European TV appearance, it was one of their first anywhere. In the past Bill Ham had always steered clear of airing his protegés on prime time television, and that despite offers from everything from *Midnight Special* to *Saturday Night Live*. The latter show featured them anyway, in a show which also featured a savagely funny parody of Linda Ronstadt. 'Oh no, what are they going to do to *us*?' Dusty pleaded in earshot of *Rolling Stone's* Kurt Loder.

ZZ's appearance was just as funny as Ms Ronstadt's, but nowhere near as cruel. It also highlighted just what an impact the li'l ol' boogie band from Texas had made on their homeland. The sketch involved the band centred around a nationwide phone in, with viewers asked to vote in a Democratic candidate for the forthcoming Presidential elections. The candidates were Walter Mondale, John Glenn, Gary Hart, Jesse Jackson, George McGovern, Cranston, Hollings, Hart and - as nominated by father Guido Sarducci (a.k.a. comedian Don Novello), three

cuddly looking Texans wearing cheap sunglasses, slouch hats and wrap-around whiskers.

Over two hundred and sixty thousand votes were called in over the next hour or so, and when they were counted up at the end of the show there was no doubting who was the people's choice. ZZ totalled 131,384 votes. Second placed Jackson finished with little more than half that: 66,968.

It was Ham who first mooted the video scheme, together with director Tim Newman. Billy told Kerrang!: 'The idea was already in the basic planning stages when we were finally called in and everyone just said 'OK! Let's do it!' So that's how we all ended up in the California desert saying 'Let's do WHAT?' You see, we'd gone headlong into the project without actually working out everything in advance. Consequently there was a lot of give-and-take, plus a lot of spontaneity about the final video. But the fundamental premise behind the storyline was that ZZ Top didn't want to play the main roles and come across as actors. We were keen

merely to be ourselves.'

The first video, shot to accompany 'Gimme All Your Loving', centred around the antics of three leggy beauties, a garage mechanic and - of course - the Eliminator. And so successful was the project, both for all involved in its creation and in terms of its commercial impact, that when ZZ convened to prepare subsequent videos, the cast and imagery remained as intact as possible. The exception was 'T.V. Dinners', a song inspired, it is said, by Dusty's habit of 'popping 'em outta the tin foil first. That's presumably what makes your skin turn blue.'

The video starred the tiny blue monster which lived in just one such TV dinner, and its predilection for watching ZZ on television. Technically, the

Below left: Big, Bad & Texan, 1983.
Below: Cheap Sunglasses.

ROSS HALFIN/REPFOTO LONDON

video was clumsy, a piece of animation created by the newly founded video department at Ardent Studios. The monster, though, was genuinely cute; the song was genuinely funny. And if 'TV Dinners' is the least remembered of the four 'Eliminator' videos, that's a fate which is due more to the startling quality of the other three films than any deficiency on the part of 'Dinners'.

Every time a new single was released, in conjunction, of course, with a new video, 'Eliminator' shot back up the U.S. album chart. By January 1, over two million copies had sold - ZZ's most successful album by far. On April 30, that total had topped three million, on August 24, it reached four million. By the end of the year, worldwide sales stood at a staggering seven and a half million, and the album had remained in the *Billboard* Top 50 for ninety weeks. The album even earned ZZ their very first Grammy nomination. Had their competition been anyone less formidable than The Police, they would probably have won that as well.

'The idea for the 'Sharp Dressed Man' video came from the credits of a movie we were

watching. Actually it was 'Sharp Eyed Man', but that didn't make any sense. You can be sharp dressed in any mode of fashion,' Billy told *Sounds*, while Dusty defined the term as 'anything I'm not wearing.'

Billy claimed that Frank was the original inspiration for the song. 'He's Rod Stewart by way of the *American Gigolo*,' he laughed. 'Yeah, the movie. I freaked over Giorgio's (Moroder) stuff and by the time everybody else was into it, I'd got the Fila kit, shirts and tennis outfits...'

In an interview with Max Bell, Frank revealed some quite surprising sartorial tastes. 'I like European clothes,' he said. 'Parisian knitwear is gorgeous - and everything Italian of course. For design I favour Cerruti and Armani. And Lois jeans. You can fit your hand in the pocket. That's the trick with jeans.'

Most successful of the four 'Eliminator' singles was 'Legs', the last of the sequence of Tim Newman directions.

Set in a shopping mall, it retained the same rock 'n' roll fantasies as its predecessors: the 'Ordinary Guy', the three beauties, the car, the magical ZZ keyring and at the back of all the action, the smiling, benevolent presence of ZZ Top.

The release of 'Legs' marked several departures from ZZ's traditional format. For a start, it was the first time any of their records had spawned four singles (even 'The Best Of ZZ Top' had retrospectively mustered only that many), it was the first time a ZZ single was released while the band were not touring, and it was the first time ZZ got into the Billboard Top 5. 'Legs' peaked at number 4 and was only prevented from hitting the top notch by the likes of Prince, Bruce Springsteen and Ray Parker Junior's startlingly successful '(Theme From) Ghostbusters'.

The element of farce present in 'Legs' exceeded both 'Sharp Dressed Man' and 'Gimme All Your Loving'. True to the song's lyrics, the video focused almost exclusively on its heroine's legs, but not only were seemingly inevitable cries of sexism conspicuous by their absence, for many people the most potent single image from the video was the revolving fluffy guitars which ZZ played.

Known to the band as Ultra-bushes, Billy had been using a fluffy guitar on and off since his days with The Moving Sidewalks. He debuted one when that band opened for The Doors in Houston, and lined it up alongside another guitar constructed from a toilet seat, the pink 'Hendrix' Stratocaster, Pearly Gates, and a host of other guitars, real or imaginary, whose reputation has made Billy's name a legend amongst serious guitar collectors.

Guitar World, in May 1984, reported that Billy owned some two hundred and seventy guitars, as well as holding nine separate patents (with two more pending) as a designer. The ZZ Top fan club marketed his renowned *Chiquita* model, claiming 'Billy designed this guitar to be a truly portable instrument...(an) excellent learning guitar for small hands and the ultimate in professional stage guitar.'

Billy began studying guitar design during his art student days at the University of Texas. 'Of course, my studies fell by the wayside as soon as music started kicking in. The Moving Sidewalks had released a couple of records that started

Above: Sharp Dressed Men.

ever, although they were originally going to be made for just a one-time usage and explode at the end.'

Another of Billy's '...customised beyond belief' guitars is a Fender Stratocaster which, *Guitar World* reported, had its entire body replaced with a replica carved and welded out of an old Model T Ford. 'I don't know if Henry Ford or Leo Fender, either one, would approve,' Billy chuckled.

Of course, Billy's collection is not limited solely to his own creations and commissions. He began collecting guitars after finding Pearly Gates. Since then he has acquired some original 1950s Gretsch guitars, from the days when the DeArmond company made their pick-ups, all the solid body Fender and Gibson offerings from the fifties and sixties, a complete set of Alamo guitars ('they play like melted butter and there are some pretty wicked shapes available'), sundry pre-war steel guitars, a few Japanese instruments 'that would do better to appear in a cartoon series' and - his pride and joy - a legendary Gibson Moderne.

According to *Guitar World*, the Moderne is 'the unicorn of collectibles', an instrument so rare that many enthusiasts prefer to plug the gap in their collection by claiming the guitar didn't even exist!

Says Billy: 'In 1957, Gibson introduced three new guitars: the Flying V, the Explorer and the Moderne. The only two to make it to the Chicago convention were the Flying V and the Explorer. Apparently they decided to pull the Moderne. Rumour has it that only about fifty of them were manufactured, but the records at Gibson are so sketchy that they're unable to confirm their whereabouts or their authenticity without actually seeing the instruments.

'I'd heard stories about the guitar long before I came across one. But finally I contacted a guy who had one. He's a player, but he didn't really like the guitar because it was unlike anything that was popular at the time. And I tell you, it's unlike anything that's popular now! But I bought it for a little bit of nothing. It had Gibson written at the top of the neck and it had two hum-bucking pick ups. That was enough for me. I remember telling

getting notoriety, so I then decided to make music a full-time endeavour. But not wanting to get too far away from my art school background, I've kept up my interest in design as well.'

These designs have seen him move from a guitar shaped like the state of Texas, employed during the 1976 tour and '...big enough to throw a dance on,' the car-shaped axes which he and Dusty played on the 'Eliminator' outing - 'the volume and tone controls were in the hubcaps. We did try having exhaust shoot out of the tail pipes, but it used to put a really weird buzz through the PA system so we had to stop' - and, on a wildly impractical, and still unfulfilled, level, a playable plexiglass guitar with a live goldfish swimming around inside. See-through guitars were also mooted as on-stage display cases for Mexican food!

'The automobile guitars were made by a guy called Wayne Charvel and they're exquisite,' Billy enthuses. 'I believe speciality instruments are created for a moment, rather than a classic for-the guy: 'Well it looks like a war club, but I'll take it.'

The guitar has no serial number, but, despite not being 'in pristine condition' and bearing scars consistent with its previous owner 'being proud of his E7th chord', the guitar's finish is still intact and, although he admits that he still can't verify the guitar's authenticity, Billy is convinced that it is the real thing.

'A couple of Gibson reps have seen it, but they're too young to have been around when it was made. So far it's never been seen by any of those Gibson people who were around in '57. But...I have every reason to believe it is a very rare instrument. I'm proud to own it.'

Doubtless he felt almost as proud when ZZ ran away with the second annual MTV Awards ceremony, held at Radio City Music Hall on September 14. In a star studded ceremony, hosted by Bette Midler and featuring an excellent impromptu lesson in guitar-smashing by Roger Daltrey, Tim Newman won the Best Director award for his work on 'Sharp Dressed Man', and ZZ Top the Best Performance by a Rock Group category with the same song. The Divine Miss M introduced the band as 'America's most lovable and mysterious rockers,' and prefaced the group's lip-synch performance of their winning number with the quip: 'No-one really knows what they look like under those beards; they may only be ten years old'. Well, fourteen years, actually, but as Dusty was said to have remarked after the ceremony: 'At least she credited us with a bit of history! Most people in New York seem to think we're a brand new band!' - or, as they heard one girl remark when ZZ appeared on the British TV show *The Tube*: 'Oh, ZZ Top? They're a fashion!'

Actually, recognition in New York had, according to Billy, come a year or so earlier. He

Below: Wheeling out the Blues: the car guitars.

REX FEATURES

told the *New Musical Express*: 'The other day one of the finest compliments was paid. We were in New York, the cab driver had his radio on and the definitive art band, The Talking Heads, I suppose the ones who have been labelled as such, the DJ said: 'Here's the Talking Heads doing their impersonation of ZZ Top.' Pull over! Stop the car! We ran around the car dancing. We've been recognised! I mean, in New York City. It was quite a moment.'

More was to come. Six weeks after the MTV award ceremony, ZZ was asked to introduce the *Friday Night Video Special*. Which they did, live from the Johnson Space Center, inside the Space shuttle. Not quite the first rock band in space, but close enough. And a week after that, ZZ burst into the most anti-rock 'n'roll homes across the nation when NBC's 'St. Elsewhere' hospital soap

opera put on a great parody of the 'Legs' video, replete with spinning Ultra Bush guitars, the ZZ girls, three Billy, Dusty and Frank lookalikes and, to top it all, a guest appearance from the *Eliminator* herself! That episode has since been nominated for an Emmy award.

ZZ's imagery even found its way on to British prime time television, via an advertisement for a leading motor manufacturer which went a long way towards borrowing its plot from the 'Gimme All Your Lovin'' video.

'We do have an image which is easy to take-off,' Billy has remarked. He told the *New Musical Express*: 'We were playing in Denver and Dusty says; 'Check row five, two o'clock.' And I looked over and there were five guys that had these pin-on beards, and they had that move we do in the video, and they were all in perfect step.'

Enjoy and Get it on

The tour over, ZZ immediately began work on the follow-up set to 'Eliminator'. The problems they faced were immeasureable: 'Eliminator' *had* been an incredibly technical album, by past standards at any rate. Add to that its astonishing popularity and it all equalled a hard act to follow.

As recording commenced, a few snippets of information did get out. Billy told *Record Mirror*: 'We were all fired up with enthusiasm after the British dates and we've been pressing on rigorously. The album's taken a long time. But we do want to learn about the new equipment... (although) ZZ Top won't be a synthesizer band. This new record will still be a rock album, and we'll continue along those lines, but we will use them.'

He revealed that he had wanted to bring in a drum machine, 'But Frank said it would take his job away so I forgot that idea.' He was proud, however, of the band's acquisiton of a Fairlight computer. 'It can produce any noise you like through a guitar, so there could be quite a few car sounds!'

Amidst all the excitement of recording the new album, though, there was still the business of promoting - and, at the request of some journalists - analysing 'Eliminator'. In that same *Record Mirror* piece, Billy said: 'I do think we're entering into a new era as far as lyrics go, and just in the last six months there's been a return to people saying, 'Let's discuss something with a bit more depth.' ZZ Top has never been a message band (as David Lee Roth once remarked: 'If you wanna send messages use Western Union!'), so for us

it's a challenge to come up with something meaningful. I think this time we've managed to capture a bit of that and discuss something different.' He admitted that in the past, even as recently as 'Eliminator', ZZ had been guilty of some sexism. But, he added, in the nicest possible way. Answering criticisms levelled at the 'Sharp Dressed Man' video, and the accusation that ZZ are simply 'plain, down-home sexists,' he agreed with all charges.

'We are, most definitely. But for 'Sharp Dressed Man' we tried to think of something typically American, and typically 'fun'. That's been the case with a lot of ZZ Top records over the years.'

And it wasn't only their music which came in for scrutiny. Frank's passion for golf, Billy's encouter with Annabella Lu Win, vocalist with Bow Wow Wow, in the Mexican desert ('I was walking down this road on my own and I saw this figure coming towards me. Got to about ten yards from each other and I recognised her. We stopped and looked at each other, then she said 'Have you got the time?' I said 'I don't believe this!' She said 'Neither do I' and we carried on walking.'), even Dusty's tattoo was deemed worthy of saturation press coverage. But there again, they were good stories - especially Dusty's

tattoo. Resplendent on his right bicep stands a buffalo, the legacy of a Tequila binge in a Mexican bar. According to *Sounds*, he only had it done because he was drunk; so drunk, in fact, that he ended up getting banned from the tattooist's parlour. From there he returned to the bar and almost got murdered by Mexicans for shouting 'Remember the Alamo!' He had a fight in the middle of the road with a taxi driver, and ended up going home with a girl whose lesbian lover, a 'bull dagger, turned up two days later and came after me with a knife.'

Dusty hit the headlines again in December. On the 16th, he was taking off his cowboy boots when the .38 Derringer pistol which he always carried around in one of them (!) fell to the ground and shot him in the abdomen. He was rushed to hospital for three hours surgery, then placed in the Critical Care unit for three days. From there he moved to a private room, and was finally discharged on Christmas Day, straight into the task of replying to the hundred thousand 'Get Well' cards and letters sent in by fans. But despite his rapid recovery, few people can be unaware of how close Dusty came to fulfilling one of his more bizarre personal ambitions; 'When I die I don't wanna be buried in a coffin. My guitar case

will suit me.'

At the time of writing, ZZ Top's tenth album, the one which will finally silence even the minority who like to believe 'Eliminator' was a one-off flash in the pan, has yet to emerge. It has no reason to. 'Eliminator' is still selling strongly, quite likely the group could retire today and live forever on the royalties not only from that particular big daddy, but also the eight records which preceded it. As a new generation is introduced to ZZ Top, what could be more natural than them wanting to come to grips with all that went before?

But ZZ won't be retiring. Not for a long while to come. It's taken them a long time to do it, but the world is now theirs for the asking. From 'Neighbour Neighbour' to 'Gimme All Your Loving', from 'Back Door Love Affair' to 'Sharp Dressed Man', ZZ have ploughed a groove through rock 'n' roll which will never be eradicated. Billy remarked, around the time of 'Eliminator', that the reason ZZ Top have been together for so long is 'because we enjoy it. That has kept us rolling right on through.'

And that, like the cars and Texas freeways, will keep them rolling on still.

Discographies

THE MOVING SIDEWALKS: singles

99th Floor*/What Are You Going To Do?*
Tantara 3101 - US only 1967

99th Floor*/What Are You Going To Do?*
Wand 1156 - US only 1967

Need Me*/Every Night A New Surprise*
Wand 1167 - US only 1967

I Want To Hold Your Hand*/Joe Blues
Tantara 3108 - US only 1968

Flashback/No Good To Cry
Tantara 3113 - US only 1969

THE MOVING SIDEWALKS: EP

99th Floor*/What Are You Going To Do?*/ Need Me*/
Every Night A New Surprise*
Movie 1030 - US only 1980

THE MOVING SIDEWALKS: LPs

FLASH
Tantara 6919 - US only 1968

FLASH
Tantara TS 6919 - US only Reissue of above 1983

99TH FLOOR
*Eva 12002 - France only Reissue of above + four non-LP
cuts as released on singles marked ***

THE CELLAR DWELLERS: singles

Bad Day/Call
Steffeck Records - US only 1968

THE WARLOCKS: singles

Splash/Life's A Mystery
Paradise 1021 - US only 1968

If You Really Want Me To Stay/Good Time Trippin'
Ara 1017 - US only 1968

THE WARLOCKS with LADY WILDE single

Another Year/Poor Kid
Ara 1915 - US only 1968

AMERICAN BLUES: single

If I Were A Carpenter/All I Saw Was You
Karma 101 - US only 1969

AMERICAN BLUES: albums

American Blues Is Here
Karma 1001 - US only 1969

American Blues Do Their Thing
Uni 73044 - US only 1970

ZZ TOP: singles

Salt Lick/Miller's Farm
Scat 45-500 - US only 1970

Salt Lick/Miller's Farm
London 45-131 - US only 1970

Shakin' Your Tree/Neighbour, Neighbour
London 45-138 - US only 1970

Francine/Francine (Spanish)
London 45-179 - US only 1972

Francine/Down Brownie
London HLU 10376 - UK only 1972

La Grange/Just Got Paid
London 45-179 - US only 1974

Beer Drinkers and Hell Raisers/La Grange
London HLU 10458 - UK only 1974

La Grange/Just Got Paid
London HLU 10475 - UK only 1974

Tush/Blue Jean Blues
London 5N-220 - US only 1975 (first US picture sleeve)

Tush/Blue Jean Blues
London HLU 10495 - UK only 1975

It's Only Love/Asleep In The Desert
London 5N-241 - US only 1976

It's Only Love/Asleep In The Desert
London HLU 10538 - UK only 1976

It's Only Love/Arrested For Driving While Blind
London 5N-251 - US only 1977

Arrested For Driving While Blind/Neighbour Neighbour
London HLU 10547 - UK only 1977

El Diablo/Enjoy And Get It On
London 5N-252 - US only 1977

I Thank You/Fool For Your Stockings
WB 49163 - US only 1980

I Thank You/Fool For Your Stockings
WB K17516 - UK only 1980

Cheap Sunglasses/Cheap Sunglasses (live)
WB 49220 - US only 1980

Cheap Sunglasses/
WB K - UK only 1980

Tube Snake Boogie/It's So Hard
WB 49865 - US only 1980

Leila/Don't Tease Me
WB 49782 - US only 1981

Gimme All Your Loving/If I Could Only Flag Her Down
WB 29693 - US only 1983

Gimme All Your Loving/If I Could Only Flag Her Down
WB W 9693 - UK only 1983

Gimme All Your Loving/Jesus Just Left Chicago/Arrested For
Driving While Blind/Heard It On The X
WB W 9693T - UK only 1983

Sharp Dressed Man/I've Got The Six
WB 29576 - US only 1983

Sharp Dressed Man/I've Got The Six
WB W9576 - UK only 1983

Sharp Dressed Man/I Got The Six/La Grange
WB W9576T - UK only 1983

La Grange/Tush
WB 0374 - US only 1984

TV Dinners/Cheap Sunglasses
WB 9334 - UK only 1984

Legs/Bad Girl
WB 29272 - US only 1984

Legs/Bad Girl
WB 9272 - UK only 1984

ZZ TOP: albums

FIRST ALBUM
: Shaking Your 'Tree/Brown Sugar/Squank/Goin' Down To
Mexico/Old Man/Neighbour Neighbour/Certified
Blues/Bedroom Thang/Just Got Back From Baby's/Backdoor
Love Affair
London PS 584 - US only 1970
WB BSK 3268 - US only 1980
WB K56601 - UK only 1980

RIO GRANDE MUD
: Francine/Just Got Paid/Mushmouth Shouting/Ko Ko
Blue/Chevrolet/Apologies To Pearly/Bar-B-Q/Sure Got Cold
After The Rain Fell/Whiskey 'n' Mama/Down Brownie
London PS 612 - US only 1972
London SHU 8433 - UK only 1972
WB BSK 3269 - US only 1980
WB K56602 - UK only 1980

TRES HOMBRES
: Waiting For The Bus/Jesus Just Left Chicago/Beer Drinkers
and Hell Raisers/Master Of Sparks/Hot Blues and
Righteous/Move Me On Down The Line/Precious and
Grace/La Grange/Sheik/Have You Heard
London PS 631 - US only 1973
London SHU 8459 - UK only 1973
WB BSK 3270 - US only 1980
WB K56603 - UK only 1980

FANDANGO
: Thunderbird/Jailhouse Rock/Backdoor Medley/Backdoor
Love Affair/Mellow Down Easy/Backdoor Love Affair
no.2/Long Distance Boogie/Nasty Dogs and Funky
Kings/Blue Jean Blues/Balinese/Mexican Bluebird/Heard It
On The X/Tush
London PS 656 - US only 1975
London SHU 8482 - UK only 1975
WB BSK 3271 - US only 1980
WB K56604 - UK only 1980

TEJAS
: It's Only Love/Arrested For Driving While Blind/El
Diablo/Snappy Kakkie/Enjoy & Get It On/10 Dollar
Man/Pan Am Highway Blues/Avalon Hideaway/She's A
Heartbreaker/Asleep In The Desert
London PS 680 - US only 1976
London LDU 1 - UK only 1976
WB BSK 3272 - US only 1980
WB K56605 - UK only 1980

BEST OF ZZ TOP
: Tush/Waiting For The Bus/Jesus Left Chicago/Francine/Just
Got Paid/La Grange/Blue Jean Blues/Backdoor Love
Affair/Beer Drinkers and Hell Raisers/Heard It On The X
London PS 706 - US only 1977
Telefunken/Nova 623361 - Germany only 1977
WB BSK 3273 - US only 1980
WB K56598 - UK only 1983

DEGUELLO
: I Thank You/She Loves My Automobile/I'm Bad, I'm
Nationwide/Fool For Your Stockings/Manic Mechanic/Dust
My Broom/Lowdown In The Street/Hi-Fi Mama/Cheap
Sunglasses/Esther Be The One
WB HS 3361 - US only 1980
WB K56701 - UK only 1980

EL LOCO
: Tube Snake Boogie/I Wanna Drive You Home/Ten Foot
Pole/Leila/Don't Tease Me/It's So Hard/Pearl
Necklace/Groovy Little Hippy Pad/Heaven, Hell Or
Houston/Party On The Patio
WB BSK 3593 - US only 1981
WB K56929 - UK only 1981

ELIMINATOR
: Gimme All Your Loving/Got Me Under Pressure/Sharp

Dressed Man/I Need You Tonight/I Got The
Six/Legs/Thug/TV Dinner/Dirty Dog/If I Could Only Flag Her
Down/Bad Girl
WB 23774-1 - US only 1983
WB W 3774 - UK only 1983

ZZ TOP PROMOTIONAL RELEASES

Singles.

All the below were released in the United States only, and all
in 12" format.

Cheap Sunglasses (Live/Studio)
(PRO 887) 1980

Gimme All Your Loving/Under Pressure
(PRO 2011) 1983

Gimme All Your Loving/Sharp Dressed Man/TV Dinners
(PRO 2094) 1983

Legs/Legs (extended mix)
(PRO 212Y) 1983

Legs/Legs (Dance Mix)
(PRO 2146) 1983

Albums

DEGUELLO
(HS 3661) - released in special outer cover

ZZ TOP LIVE
(King Biscuit Flour Hour) 1980: 2 LP/3 sided live album

RETNA

ACKNOWLEDGEMENTS

For quotes and other information used in the text I would like to thank the following: John Williams, Robert Christgau, Barney Hoskins, Simon Hills, Max Bell, Chet Flippo, Richard Grabel, Malcolm Dome, Garry Bushell, Chris Charlesworth, Peter Crescenti, Gordon Fletcher, Dave Thomas, *Custom Car, Modern Drummer, Guitar World* and *Record Collector.*

Special thanks to Jo-Ann Greene.

Dave Thomas, 1985